Guerrilla
Parenting

Debra dawn,
I'm thrilled to give this
book on behalf of Bing+
Michelle.
Enjoy!

The Unconventional Methods of Teaching
Your Kids Self-Reliance and How to Make Money

Guerrilla Parenting

How To Raise An
Entrepreneur

By the Former CEO of Guerrilla Marketing

David T. Fagan & Jill E. Fagan

On the Inside Press
Beverly Hills, CA

Guerrilla Parenting: How To Raise An Entrepreneur

Copyright © 2014 by David T. Fagan & Jill E. Fagan

www.DavidTFagan.com
david@davidtfagan.com

Published by On the Inside Press
Beverly Hills, CA 90210
www.OntheInsidePress.com

LCCN 2015901776
ISBN 978-0-9891625-8-6

Cover design by David T. Fagan and Carli Smith

Printed in the United State of America.

Crim22, Gar12.5, TNR, FG10

This book is dedicated to our parents,

Vernon and Lenora Fagan

and

Bruce and Jody Packard,

who raised us to be
the people we are today.

Table of Contents

Author's Note

This book was designed to be a fast read, and early feedback shows that the book can be read in two to four hours. We know parents are busy people, so we wrote the book to keep things moving quickly.

It starts with parenting insights, ideas, and solutions. There are a ton of interactive activities you can do with your kids and very specific conversations you should have with them as well. The book also has a test in the middle that can be very revealing in regards to whether or not you are more of an Average Parent or a Guerrilla Parent.

Next are very detailed business plans for you and your kids to consider. These plans include everything from a supply list, scripts, and ads to safety tips, appropriate age groups, and money that could be made. We also talk specifically about how our kids have made most of their money.

At the end, my wife and I put an About the Authors section if you want to know more about us. There are some key milestones in our lives and what some of our accomplishments have been. This is not designed to be a bragging session; rather we discuss both our successes (like our businesses) as well as our failures (like losing everything in 2007 and camping out for a summer).

Make sure to read the Introduction in detail. It's important. There are also a lot of images throughout the book that can be helpful in raising a child to be an entrepreneur or a self-reliant adult. You can download these images for easier viewing and printing at www.GuerrillaParenting.com/teachingtools.

Also realize that the words 'I' and 'we' are used fairly interchangeably. I, David, am doing most of the writing with Jill's thoughts and ideas mixed in.

Enjoy!

David T. Fagan
Jill E. Fagan

Introduction

You need to know what kind of book this is and what kind of book this isn't. This isn't a textbook for schools, although we know several educators that would like to see it taught publicly. It's not a clinical book either; after all, we are not doctors of any sort. It's also not a bragging session because our kids have had some success. You might even be wondering what qualifies us to write a book on raising self-reliant individuals or, in many cases, entrepreneurs.

After all, I left high school in the beginning of the 11th grade and got my GED. Later I went to the University of Phoenix with my employer reimbursing most costs, but I never graduated from there either. I even took some Harvard courses in Boston designed for CEO's, but I obviously didn't graduate from Harvard.

What I have learned how to do is to study good books, recruit great mentors, take specific classes for specific purposes, and customize my education as needed. This has led me to a fair amount of success, as well as some amount of failure too.

My wife Jill is very different, graduating from high school as an A and B student and then going to college on a full scholarship. Where I mostly read for a purpose, Jill reads for sport – even rereading some of her favorite books.

I love to coach kids and have coached many youth sports teams. I run teen entrepreneur conferences and summer camps, and all my kids regularly make money working. I run a marketing and media company, calling my sailboat that's docked two miles from our Laguna home in California my main office.

Jill runs her own boutique publishing company helping experts and authors tell their stories, but she is always a mother first.

Both of our parents are still married with 85 years of combined anniversaries. Jill is the middle of eight kids and I am the oldest of six. We have nine children and are currently raising eight, ages 3-17. We have four girls and four boys. This is not said to qualify us as parenting experts. Rather it's to let you know where we are coming from and what our life experiences are.

We believe you have to...

1. Parent in an age appropriate way.
2. Parent every child a little differently because every child is at least a little different.
3. Delegate, defer, and even drop other activities in order to take time being a good parent.
4. Avoid giving your child too much.
5. Let your children fail from time to time.
6. Let your kids experience the natural consequences of their actions most of the time.
7. Protect your kids from habit forming distractions.
8. Creatively discipline your kids.
9. Foster independence in your children.
10. Teach your kids ways to make money.
11. Teach your children how to take care of themselves.
12. Show your child how to serve others unconditionally.
13. Show your kids how to invest in themselves and handle money.
14. Teach your children to have healthy relationships.
15. Teach your kids to overcome their fears.
16. Help your children develop their talents.

One of the most important things we believe is that you can't take all the blame for your children's mistakes, just as you can't take all the credit for their talents and successes. Sometimes our children need to just figure things out the hard way on their own. Other times our children succeed no matter how poorly we parented.

In our businesses we coach people daily. We work to inspire people, instruct dreamers, course correct action takers, and help people monetize their knowledge and experiences. Everything we teach our clients we teach our kids. You might say that we truly practice at home what we preach every day in the world.

I've helped kids break records, write books, start businesses, make money, and fulfill dreams. Nothing has ever made me happier than doing these things. Writing this book has helped me probably as much as it can help you as a parent.

You will learn parenting problems you may not have even known you had, as well as parenting solutions you never knew were possible. Either way, this is not a conventional parenting book rehashing average parenting tips. Instead, this is an unconventional parenting book teaching you how to teach your kids to become self-reliant and make money doing something that they will love whenever possible.

For more on us read, the About the Authors section in the back of the book.

THIS IS THE START OF WISDOM
THAT SOME TRUTHS HAVE GREATER VALUE.

Chapter 1
Problems with Parenting

All sane people love their children. Every parent wants to see their kids succeed and be happy. Of course, this is easier said than done due to the vast amount of variables in raising children. I'm not just talking about nature versus nurture. Homes, neighborhoods, schools, budgets, and time available can all differ quite a bit when it comes to the things we are slightly more likely to control as parents.

Conventional knowledge has become the belief parents should start enrolling kids in school systems as young as possible; pack their schedules full of sports, music, and homework; sacrificing at all costs to get them into a good college where they will get a degree and then magically become employed, successful, and ultimately happy.

Today's conventional approach came from a more internal instinct with wanting our children to be able to take care of themselves. For thousands of years, if not longer, education has been key to survival and success. For hundreds of years, if not longer, traditional colleges and universities have had somewhat of a monopoly on teaching young people what to learn and how to excel in various fields. This has led to a great push for higher education, attendance at the best schools, and the desire for advanced degrees.

Unfortunately, this push is now pulling parents and their children into greater debt with degrees and an overall education that is not paying off. Student loans are now the second highest

5

debt in the United States behind home loans with a growing number of graduates not even using their degrees and living at home with parents.

"Many people die at 25 and aren't buried until they are 75."
~ Benjamin Franklin

Now you might be thinking that I am anti college, but that isn't true. I just don't believe everyone is meant to go to traditional colleges no matter the cost and that in order to be good parents you have to pay for your kids' tuition. This college craze has become the tail wagging the dog. Priorities are getting out of order, and parents as a whole are losing track of what matters most…teaching your kids to become self-reliant.

Of course, this belief is unconventional, and that's why I call it Guerrilla Parenting. The guerrilla approach is all about the unconventional way of reaching conventional goals. I know that our parenting style isn't for everyone. It may not even be for most people, but that's the problem with schools today: they cannot afford to cater to the minority learning styles in a class room. Most schools focus on the majority in every way.

Just like every sane parent loves their child, every sane teacher loves their student. Unfortunately teachers are stuck in a system that is not easy to change, and they are not rewarded for the success of the individual; rather they are incentivized on the scores of the majority if they are incentivized at all.

You need to know that this book is about so much more than the broken school system, but I mention it all the same because it is potentially a parent's greatest problem. As a society, we have allowed schools to become this way because so many people don't know how to parent, don't want to parent, or can't or won't make time to parent.

So as a default, the government and schools are now trying to parent for us. They tell us what is most important for our kids to learn, how to discipline them, and they will fill up the majority of our children's time if we let them.

Again, just like all sane parents love their kids and all sane teachers love their students, all sane government leaders love the youth. But this isn't a book about questioning sane people's love and hope for children. It's about the best way for you to teach your child self-reliance…and how to maybe even become an entrepreneur.

So if the school system and government aren't your child's greatest problem on the path to success, then what is? It's you. You are your child's greatest problem, as well as its greatest promise and potential for success in life. Of course our problem as parents is that we are typically ill equipped and under educated when it comes to parenting.

More specific problems parents face are:

1. Every child is different.
2. Almost every form of music, movies, television, and the internet are working against you.
3. Many parents are raising at least one child by themselves.

4. Many parents are raising a child where the other parent has different ideas on parenting.
5. There are a lot of things stimulating your child's mind and competing for its time and attention.
6. You have bad parenting habits that are hard to break.
7. Your kids have bad habits that are hard to break.

You are more powerful than you know and some fear the day you discover it.

I could go on, but I don't want to discourage you. Of course I write that somewhat jokingly, but there is hope. A different mindset, an unconventional approach, and consistent follow through can change almost everything.

In the end, your child's success will be up to them. After all, they have their free agency to choose as they wish. This might be the hardest part for parents: learning to live with their children's choices. But good parents learn how to do just that.

Many parents are now easily spending $1,000 or more on their kids' birthday parties (or worse they spend money they don't even have). They value friendship with their children more than leadership for their children. And most parents now believe they have to pay for their kids' college education in order to be good, successful parents. The result seems to be kids growing up slowly these days with many adult children living at home with their parents for years and years.

This is the second time I have brought up grown adult children living with parents, so I should say that without a shadow of a doubt there are several good reasons for children to live with their parents for limited periods of time. There is nothing wrong with children living with parents in general either.

Unfortunately, it's these good reasons stemming from genuine need that regularly disguise the bad reasons of laziness and enabled mediocrity. Parents must know that in many cases they create the bad reasons and are not helping by hiding the real reasons their grown, adult children still live with them.

I believe almost all parents are acting out of love with their hearts in the right place. Yet, ironically they are giving their kids everything, which more than ever, means having their adult children end up with nothing.

Here are 8 Ways to Avoid Condemning Your Kids to a Life of Mediocrity:

1. Teach Self-Reliance – It used to be that as a society and as parents we focused more on self-reliance. We wanted our children to grow up and be able to take care of themselves, having their own lives and fulfilling their own dreams in their pursuit of happiness. Help your children develop a work ethic and take care of themselves. Quite simply, we need to teach them to recognize what they want and truly need, and then teach them how to get it for themselves whenever possible.

2. Customize their Education – Mark Twain said, "Never let schooling get in the way of your education." It's your job as a parent to help your children discover their talents and to develop them through practice, hard work, and involvement in strategic activities. Enable them to take the classes and experience the real life situations that will help them grow as individuals. Scouting is still one great organization out there that helps with this more than anything else I know of. Still,

this is your responsibility as a parent more than anyone else in the world.

3. <u>Focus on Getting Results</u> – More than anything, employers want people who can get results and show a positive contribution. Yes, many places require a degree, but even if they get that job they have to think, act, and get things done on their own. The real trend in the marketplace is the growing need for small business owners and entrepreneurs. Along with Dr. Kenneth Lewis Sr., I agree that this is the Era of the Entrepreneur. It has never been a better time to work for yourself, but you have to know how to get results. Help your children focus on what information and skills they need to do specific jobs.

4. <u>College is NOT for Everyone</u> – Give your kids all the options. Somewhere along the way, colleges and universities started cornering the market on higher education with the best chance of giving our children an advantage. I firmly believe this monopoly on education must be broken, and we are seeing the cracks now. We must stop worshipping the false god of college. You may even want to invest in a business for your kids before a traditional college education. Instead of spending $50,000 to $200,000 on college, spend $5,000 on helping them start their own business. I refuse to save for my kids' college or create a belief in my home that college will be covered. They can earn good grades and scholarships, take out some loans, get assistance from an employer, or even join the military.

5. <u>Let your Kids Fail</u> – Parent by the natural consequences. If they don't do their homework, sometimes you have to let them receive the appropriate grade. The simple fact is that most kids, and people in general for that matter, don't learn what they are capable of until they have to learn what they are capable of. This journey is the real education that leads to self-

reliance, yet most parents steal this priceless experience from their children almost daily.

6. <u>Don't Rescue Your Kids</u> – No one likes to see their kids be mistreated. Kids will be picked on and bullied by people of all shapes, sizes, and gender. Although there are times to take matters into your own hands, most kids will be better off in the long run if you help them to learn to deal with being treated unfairly or with cruelty. We can't always be there with them every second of the day so let them do what they can on their own. There are a lot of learning opportunities especially for teenagers in this area of their life.

7. <u>Challenge Your Kids</u> – Find things that they like or love and together create challenging goals for them to reach. Make it within their grasp and age appropriate, but challenge them all the same. They need to see progress and the power they have to make things happen for themselves. They can learn that in many ways they are in control of their own destiny.

8. <u>Love Them No Matter What</u> – Compliment your kids regularly and let them know you love them. People call me the meanest dad in the world, but every one of my kids knows I love them. Guerrilla Parenting requires tough choices, sometimes going without, sometimes letting your kids watch from the sidelines, and this only works with a lot of love. They must know what is most important in life, and you must show them and remind them whenever possible.

Children that have everything given to them don't necessarily end up poor or in jail. They just end up with mediocre lives where they never really reach their full potential.

Are you, as a parent, going to save, rescue, and pay for everything for most of your kids' lives or are you going to lead, inspire, and provide a path for your child to walk towards greatness? You're the parent and it's up to you, no one else.

Chapter 2
The Whatever Epidemic

"Whatever Mom. Whatever Dad. Just Whatever." The phrase whatever says so much about our society. I suppose the attitude of whatever has been around and growing for some time now. If you don't know what this phrase really means, either because you no longer speak teen or you never really did in the first place, I will now translate it for you.

Whatever essentially means, "Mom and Dad, I have so many nice things in my life that I couldn't care less about what you think, and I don't mind telling you so. Nothing you can say or do will really affect me or my course of actions. What you are saying and doing have no real impact on my ability to continue to enjoy life as I now know it."

Yes, the phrase whatever means all that…and maybe even a little more.

I believe most Whatever Epidemic cases are curable with consistent doses of what I call "prosperity reduction", but I am getting ahead of myself. First let's talk about what causes the most severe cases and what the symptoms are.

Did you know that the average school age kid has over $2,000 worth of their own technology at their fingertips? Just research the numbers of kids that have phones, tablets, laptops, computers, televisions, and game console systems. What's even crazier is that by my estimation every two years almost all of the technology is updated!

The material possessions of school age children does not stop there. These numbers don't account for scooters, bicycles, skateboards, rollerblades, balls, hoops, goals, clubs, bats, tennis tables, pool tables, ping pong tables, board games, remote control vehicles, trampolines, dolls, random toys, and swimming pools!

> The average child has more than $2,000 of their own technology that is replaced every two years.

None of these things by themselves are bad in nature. Actually, most can be very rewarding. The point being made here is that our children are blessed with quite a bit to occupy their time. Most of our children live a life of comfort and good fortune, especially if we compare them to previous generations. Many other countries and cultures also know nothing of our extravagance.

Again, I have nothing against any of these things individually, but we need to help our children earn these things, take care of these things, and appreciate these things as much as possible.

As much as I hate to start a sentence with, "When I was growing up…", when I was growing up you just didn't have that many options, and the generation before me had even less to entertain themselves with.

Kids catch the Whatever Epidemic when they have too much and they feel that no matter what they temporarily lose they will still have something else to enjoy in the meantime. Most kids have no fear of loss, or at least not a fear of losing so much that it will really have an impact on the level of comfort they have grown accustomed to.

So why do parents give so much to their children to the point of infecting them with a Whatever attitude? I suppose its innocent acts filled with good intentions. What I have found is that most over-giving comes from two types of parents. It's those that "missed out" and those that are "keeping up".

"Missed Out" parents went through hard and terrible times as children, and they vowed that their kids would have more than they did growing up. A worthy and common goal with the best of intentions. For these parents there is a fear that their children will suffer in some way. Unfortunately, so much of what made the "missed out" parents so great is that they wanted something badly enough that they were willing to work hard to get it.

Ironically, their kids want for very little and have caught the Whatever virus. After all, why should they work or listen to others? Their comfort level is so high that not much matters.

"Keeping Up" parents had the best of everything, and it is almost a tradition to keep giving to their kids at the highest levels, just "keeping up". For these parents it's about pride as much as anything else. These kids get a lot of gifts and the best of everything, once again taking away the desire that comes from wanting and needing something of their own. Unfortunately, these are the parents that can typically afford what kids need most but don't always get. Most of the time these kids would be just as happy with more of their parent's time.

It's good for your children to want! You want your children to want! The attitude of not caring, not listening, and not obeying so often comes from not wanting anything. When kids want, they have to be willing to do something, learn something, and maybe even work for something.

One of a Guerrilla Parent's most primary roles is to help children learn what they want, to help them want the right things, and to show them how to get what they want. It's a paradigm shift from conventional parenting to unconventional parenting that changes everything. Your children will listen more, respond more, and work more when you help them want and act upon those worthy wants.

This can be as simple as having a child as young two years old ask others for what they want. It's common for young children to be shy and not want to talk to grownups. As soon as my children are walking and talking, they are required to ask for what they want. This is all about getting them to do things outside their current comfort zone. Guerrilla Parents teach their kids from a young age to be willing to do things that they don't want to do even if it's hard or uncomfortable.

This simple lesson pays off exponentially in life as your children grow to take on other fears and stressful situations. Teaching your kids that they can do and endure hard things is priceless and is best taught as young as possible.

My three oldest teenage daughters recently wanted to go visit my wife's parents for spring break. This meant traveling from southern California to Flagstaff, Arizona and they wanted to do it by train.

My father-in-law, Bruce, a great man, had been suffering from cancer and the treatments that accompany it. This trip was a worthy want for sure. Although probably shocking to many, I told my daughters that they needed to earn the money to go. Actually, each of them already had some money from previous entrepreneur activities and savings, but they would need to earn more for the train ticket and money to spend on the trip.

They worked together to do an enchilada sale (one of the many business plans at the back of the book). They sold about 40 dozen enchiladas to local businesses in 24 hours. It turned out that the youngest of them was the best sales girl, so her sisters recruited her to sell all 40 dozen. The others preferred to do the shopping or actual preparation of the food. They knew where each of their strengths laid and used it to their advantage.

I'll never forget being concerned that Nyah, the youngest, was just busy talking on the phone while her older sisters were working on making the enchiladas. My wife informed me that Nyah had already sold 39 dozen and that she was working the phones to sell the last dozen. Not stopping until she hit that 40 mark.

Needless to say, I was deeply impressed and extremely pleased. From that day on, the older teenage girls, Jordan and Taylor, have Nyah sell almost everything they can. There is a cute factor that helps when children are younger that diminishes as teens age. Funny I know, but it's true.

My daughters will never forget working together to earn the money for a train ride to see their grandparents knowing that they did it all by themselves. This is age appropriate self-reliance and Guerrilla Parenting at its best.

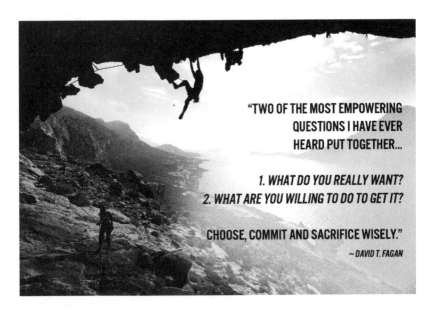

"TWO OF THE MOST EMPOWERING
QUESTIONS I HAVE EVER
HEARD PUT TOGETHER...

1. WHAT DO YOU REALLY WANT?
2. WHAT ARE YOU WILLING TO DO TO GET IT?

CHOOSE, COMMIT AND SACRIFICE WISELY."
~ DAVID T. FAGAN

It would have been fine and good for me to fund the trip, but it was even better to have them earn it. Guerrilla Parenting goes for better.

My daughter, Taylor, also earned money to go to Peru with her grandparents when she was 14. She worked hard to come up with the $1,800 needed but fell short by almost $700. I told her to make me a proposal, which is something we teach in our home.

Tell me what you want, what you need, why it's so important to you, why it should be important to me, what you have already done or what you are currently doing to get it yourself, and what you are further willing to do to get it.

My kids have gotten pretty good at the art of "The Pitch". Sometimes I even get a full blown presentation, which is what I prefer knowing that this skill and process will be valuable to them in the future.

I was sold on Taylor's current effort, impressed by what she had already made, and I agreed that it would be a highly rewarding trip. She really played to my sense of adventure and the value I put on experiencing life to the fullest.

I agreed to fund the rest of the trip with her promise to pay me back after returning home. She understood the commitment, enjoyed every minute of that 10 day trip, and returned home to pay back every penny in just a few short months.

My daughter, Nyah, recently earned money through Craigslist reselling, babysitting, and enchilada sales to come on a two week business trip with me to Australia. She had to come up with almost $1,500 and did it at age 13. (All these business plans are in the back of the book.)

Have your kids pitch you, reward effort, and make up the difference whenever possible just be careful not to set the tone that they never have to make the money up front. There are other times and trips that my kids have fallen short and they had to miss out on the opportunity.

> There are times my kids have fallen short of their goal and had to miss out on opportunities.

Those moments are heart breaking but necessary for your children to learn life's harder lessons and the emphasis that the world puts on results. Guerrilla Parents are willing to let their kids miss out, go without, and sit it out on the sidelines from time to time.

Watch out for the words and attitudes of the Whatever Epidemic. Be careful how much you give. Be willing to reduce your child's prosperity. Look for worthy wants and help them acquire and achieve as much as possible on their own.

Chapter 3
The Ambition Battle

The most frustrating thing a parent might ever face is when their child's intelligence seems to be a secret and the child could care less. This is similar to the Whatever Epidemic with its own nuances. The Whatever attitude generally results from something negative happening that the kid refuses to respond to. The Ambition Battle comes from the lack of desire for anything positive that requires overcoming consistent challenges.

Although motivation comes from each of us individually and internally, regardless of others, an inspiring environment can be the difference maker we all need. That goes double for our kids. In other words, we can't truly motivate or make anyone do anything, but creating the right surroundings can help people act upon feelings of inspiration.

Like most things in life, there are no silver bullets when it comes to parenting. All we can do is play the odds with Guerrilla Parenting best practices. The advantages we have over governments, schools, and friends is that we have the best opportunities to know our children through spending quality time in quality places doing quality activities.

This time must be spent determining and developing our child's talents. Although every potential talent discovered won't strike you rich in parenting rewards, it's only a matter of time before you strike gold hammering out a real passion of your child. Every child has one. You just have to mine it out from deep inside.

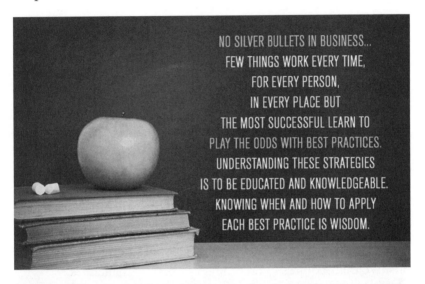

NO SILVER BULLETS IN BUSINESS... FEW THINGS WORK EVERY TIME, FOR EVERY PERSON, IN EVERY PLACE BUT THE MOST SUCCESSFUL LEARN TO PLAY THE ODDS WITH BEST PRACTICES. UNDERSTANDING THESE STRATEGIES IS TO BE EDUCATED AND KNOWLEDGEABLE. KNOWING WHEN AND HOW TO APPLY EACH BEST PRACTICE IS WISDOM.

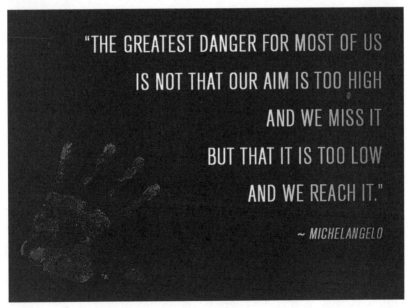

"THE GREATEST DANGER FOR MOST OF US IS NOT THAT OUR AIM IS TOO HIGH AND WE MISS IT BUT THAT IT IS TOO LOW AND WE REACH IT."

~ MICHELANGELO

Bring a pick and maybe even some dynamite because some kids like to see you work for it. As a matter of fact, the super smart kids pick up pretty quickly when they know you want something from them. A switch flips and then they like to push your buttons as you just try to help them out. Oh the joys of parenting!

Hence the Ambition Battle.

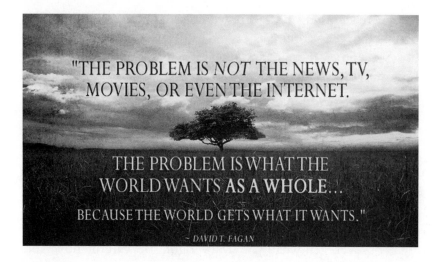

"THE PROBLEM IS *NOT* THE NEWS, TV, MOVIES, OR EVEN THE INTERNET.

THE PROBLEM IS WHAT THE WORLD WANTS **AS A WHOLE...**

BECAUSE THE WORLD GETS WHAT IT WANTS."

~ DAVID T. FAGAN

That's what I like about Scouting for both boys and girls. They have discovered the secret art of tricking kids into learning things by making it fun, adventurous, and visibly rewarding. Kids respond more to the metaphors of life found in activities rather than plain words that you have placed before them. Sports and music activities can do the same thing.

As a parent, you can rarely be the expert. Good teachers, coaches, and youth leaders can be used to your advantage.

I remember teaching one of my daughters the correct way to shoot a free throw in basketball. I must have shot thousands of free throws with her, personally showing her the best way and asking her to do it the right way another hundred times. She did well and tried her best, but I'll never forget the day she came home from a camp and said the coach taught her how to shoot a good free throw.

I bit my tongue, smiled, and congratulated her. On the inside I wanted laugh, cry, and scream. Of course I learned a valuable lesson in parenting: sometimes we need advice and instruction to come from other trusted experts. That's fine, and knowing this can give you the upper hand in inspiring your children to be better.

There's nothing quite as powerful as quoting and referencing people that they admire as examples of what you want them to do. Sometimes these examples are hard to find, granted, but opportunities are out there.

Here are two things you never want to do when fighting the Ambition Battle:

1. Never Nag – Pestering your child with your ideas, wants, and needs from them is never good. It's a very negative energy or negative spirit that typically brings out the worst in kids. It can make them feel like a failure, unloved, and useless to try because they can't ever get what you want right. Be careful how you balance the need for intense conversations with the opportunities to keep the discussion more light and positive. However, there are times for both.

2. Never Compare – This seems like one everyone would know, yet it still happens all the time. Parents not only compare their own kids to each other publicly, but also compare their kids to other parents' kids. Many times parents do this without even knowing it. This not only makes children feel bad but it can make them have negative feelings toward their siblings or friends.

I have a son that has this challenge, this lack of ambition. His IQ is the highest of all my kids, not that I put that much stock in IQ tests. He completes things fast, is very creative, and has a strong sense of what is right, wrong, and fair.

Many times he has to be convinced of things, likes to debate, and doesn't seem to be driven towards much. Of course the difference maker for him has been me spending time with him. It shouldn't be shocking that the more time I spend with him, the better he does in almost everything. The same is true for all my children, but it's especially true for him.

The more time I spend with him, the more I realize what he likes and wants. The more I discover his likes and wants, the better I understand his talents and what he is drawn to. I help him try new things like working with me in my business, going to the gym, and playing sports.

The more we try, the more we practice, and the more time we spend together the more ambition I see growing in him.

Every person and parent should be worried about addictions. Extreme addictions can be things like alcohol, drugs, or even pornography in this day and age. I think this is more common knowledge and there is a lot of education warning parents and children about these risks.

Other than the obvious health risks, the problem with addictions is that they start to rule your life by affecting your decision making. An addict's decisions are all made with their addiction in mind. Everything takes a back seat to what they crave most. They can literally lose control of everything.

Unlike additions, which we are always on the lookout for, not every person or parent is worried about distractions. A distraction is something that takes us away from real life or more serious and important daily activities. Distractions are not necessarily bad in and of themselves. In some cases distractions are good for us as a way to unwind, relax, and take a break from more stressful

> *W*e should worry about distractions as much as we do addictions.

situations. Distractions, like addictions, can also seriously alter our decision making abilities in a very negative way.

So what are the distractions that can keep our children from greatness? Video games, social media, movies, television shows, and even some degree of playing sports and playing music. You have to decide as a parent for each of your kids at what point these activities begin to be unbalanced or start to distract from other worthy life priorities. An unhealthy distraction can kill your kid's ambition for other worthy pursuits.

You have to decide at what point your child has an unusual amount of talent in an area and that you want to skew the majority of your child's time towards mostly one area of life. It's a huge decision and an exception to the rule if you're trying to help your kid have a balanced life.

Either way, be aware of distractions. If your kids don't study because they "have" to play video games this is bad. If your kids won't practice playing the piano because it's easier to watch television this is bad. If your kids don't want to play sports because they would rather just read all the time this isn't good either.

As your children become teenagers, you also have the distractions of hanging out with friends. They may rather be with some boy or girl than be at practice, working a job, or studying. Most of the time, these are just plain and simple distractions that take our children off course, deflating any ambition for meaningful pursuits.

Don't let your children become addicted to the easy way.

Watch for these warning signs of your kids wanting to spend too much time in one area of life doing less important activities and sacrificing more important opportunities to grow.

Here are some things I do and have done to reduce distractions in my kids' lives:

1. Homework, exercise, and physical play come before technology time.
2. Kids must read certain books, earn money, and do certain jobs before they can buy or have certain types of technology.
3. My teenagers don't date until they're 16, and even then they must double date with at least one more couple.
4. My dating age kids can't date the same person more than twice in a row. After the second date, they have to date someone else so they meet more people and they aren't as likely to become a couple.
5. I reward my kids for developing talents, getting good grades, and making money on their own.
6. We have tech-free weekends and weeks.
7. No tech is allowed alone in a bedroom.

While spending time with one of my daughters when she was 10, I was telling her all about New York City and how amazing it was. I got her excited about the possibilities of this fantastic place just a plane ride away. She wanted to come with me on my next trip.

I explained that she would need to earn the money. We talked about how much she would need and what she could do to earn that money. I explained how some kids made money and taught her one way people start businesses is improving upon already existing businesses.

I explained how people have car washes in public areas and then suggested we improve upon that idea by going door to door washing cars for donations. She was in. We got a bucket on wheels, some soap, some sponges, and a squeegee that she could roll up to every door.

I gave her a script of what to say. We practiced the script, and then I drove alongside her as she went door to door with her sisters offering to wash peoples' cars. Most people never answered. Many that did said, "No thanks." But when she did get a yes she just beamed with excitement. I would then hop out and help her wash the car.

Start where you are. Use what you have. Do what you can.

The first Saturday we tried this she made over $230, and she earned every penny since it was in the Arizona heat at over 100 degrees most the day. She was empowered seeing her potential. Going on that trip to NYC changed her for the better. She started dreaming bigger, and her ambition was growing. Everything seemed more possible to her.

Something magically happens when your kids have a worthy want, they know how to reach their goal, and they take the action necessary on their own to make their dreams come true.

Guerrilla Parents encourage ambition and destroy distractions whenever possible.

Chapter 4
Discipline

The simple fact is that all children will be disobedient from time to time...some more than others for sure. Children need to learn many things, even if some are as basic as being safe. Every parent wants their children to learn different things in different ways, but there must be discipline.

Talk about unconventional. Holding kids responsible, spanking, disciplining in age appropriate ways, and placing restrictions is getting pretty rare these days. I know some discipline may have been excessive in past generations, but it seems the pendulum has maybe swung too far the other way.

Because kids personalities differ so much and situations can have such a diverse set of circumstances, Guerrilla Parents must get creative in their discipline. They should be careful not to decide these punishments while being too angry. Before they make their verdict known they should also know a few things.

> *Guerrilla Parents must get creative in their discipline.*

1. <u>Never Forget the Lesson You are Trying to Teach</u> – In all your creativity and anger, be careful not to forget the issue at hand. In other words make sure the punishment fits the crime. The idea is to make sure that there is a loss of something and that it helps the child remember not to make the mistake again. They

also need to learn that in life there are consequences to our actions.

2. The Child's Age is Important – Age really matters when taking into account attention span, understanding of situations, what will be remembered most, and what might matter the most to them.

3. Avoid Limiting Good Things – Grounding from sports, music practice, church activities, and family time should obviously be avoided but you would be surprised how much this happens. I'm still surprised schools continue to suspend kids from school as punishment!

4. Find Things that are Meaningful – The prosperity reduction must be meaningful. Taking away phones, computers, television, movies, books, video games, and playing with friends can all be a good start. This is one of my favorites as kids get older.

5. Corporal Punishment – Pushups, sit-ups, jumping jacks, and laps around the block can all be good within reason. My kids always impress teachers in PE with their ability to do pushups. These exercises are not designed to make kids puke or faint. It's not even for punishment so much as it is to get their attention.

6. Allowing the Natural Consequences – Let your kids face the music of not getting their homework done, hitting a certain grade, or completing a project. They may not get the reward of the class, have to sit on the sideline, or otherwise go without. They also may end up having to do detention.

7. Doing Additional Chores – Doing jobs around the house is a good way to get things done, but be careful because you can make them hate certain jobs even more than usual.

8. <u>Restitution and Apologies are Necessary</u> – Help your kids make their wrongs right whenever possible. They need to answer to others as well. This needs to be a part of discipline.

9. <u>Your Kids Must Know You Love Them</u> – No matter how you discipline, it will always be more effective when your children know you love them a lot and love them unconditionally.

As a kid I was spanked, got grounded, and even got the belt, but always knew my parents loved me. I was never beaten, and I became a better person for the discipline I received.

The worst was when my dad would send me to my room to think about whatever I did wrong before he would later come in to spank me. The waiting was terrible! Who else put on more than one pair of pants?

My dad always came in calm, told me why I was being spanked, and then carried out the punishment. Many times later that same day if not sooner he would tell me that he still loved me and always would. I suppose that is a little old school these days and outlawed in most states, but it worked for me.

I also remember a time where I got in trouble for talking too much in class. I not only got in trouble at home but my dad took me to see the teacher to make sure I apologized face to face. I think the first time that happened was when I was only eight or nine years old.

Of course I have never spanked my kids with anything but my hand, but I have always tried to do the same thing: to carry out discipline without anger and tell my kids I love them no matter what. Easier said than done, I know.

Jill's favorite form of discipline is pushups. I think there are some days she doles out a couple hundred pushups in an afternoon…but then again we do have a few kids so they can add up fast.

> Carry out discipline without anger. Otherwise it's just punishment.

She also loves giving out jobs. Even when she grounds kids from technology, she typically gives them ways to shorten the punishment by doing extra jobs. She will also typically help the punished kid with the job as well. I suppose it's her way of letting our misbehaving child know that she still loves them and will help them. She only helps if they are working hard and not complaining.

Jill will also stay up 'til late hours of the night helping kids with school work and projects they should have done sooner. I must have helped at least once in a situation like this, but I honestly can't remember a specific time. Several times I have asked Jill about letting them face the natural consequences of their actions by going to school with their work undone.

It's hard for me or any parent to do this, but it is definitely harder for my wife and some other parents. Regardless, if you bail them out, history has shown that they will keep expecting to be bailed out and let off. This is tough love and this is Guerrilla Parenting.

Sometimes kids don't care what a class thinks, what their grade is, or how a teacher feels so there also has to be other discipline besides the natural consequences. Either way letting your child face the music is important.

I'm also a big believer in "trust but verify". I have no problem with checking my kid's texts, social media accounts, and all other forms of communication. It's more of spot checking really, but it needs to be done. You have to know where your kid is and what they're doing as much as you possibly can.

This is not a part of any punishment. This is just a part of good parenting. The expectation is set from the time they get phones or log in to Instagram that this monitoring will happen.

It's also part of the technology contract they sign and that we enforce. There have been several situations that I was able to address early on because I was active in my kids' lives.

I think there was a time when parents cared more about their kids growing up to become good people who made morally conscious decisions than anything else. Nowadays, it would appear that most parents just want their kids to be happy at all costs. These things may sound similar but they really aren't.

Being a good person and even a self-reliant person means doing things that don't always make us happy, especially in the short term. It means making sacrifices, thinking about others, having a moral compass, and working hard and sometimes long hours. Guerrilla Parents might be kind of old fashion in this way.

We must teach our kids courage. C.S. Lewis said, "Courage is not simply one of the virtues, but the form of every virtue at the testing point."

We want our kids to follow their dreams and live an on-purpose life. We want them to be self-reliant and experience love, life, and adventure. This does not mean being a millionaire, nor does it mean being perfect or self-righteous. It just means that they make the most out of what has been given to them and that they are good to those around them, bringing out the best in others. This is long term happiness and peace of mind.

Chapter 5
Work Ethic

No matter what your child does, they must have a great work ethic. They must be willing to put in the time, practice, prepare, and focus for long periods of time. Talent and love for something is good, but it has been proven time and time again that those that work the hardest will typically prevail.

This is why ambition matters so much. This is why distractions must be removed or carefully balanced at best. Every time my kids tell me they like something I say, "Well, if you really want to be good at that you just need to practice. Perfect practice makes perfect," which is part of a Vince Lombardi quote.

I said that the other day to one of my sons in front of his friends. He turned to the rest of them and said, "He always says that." They all smiled…and so did I!

One of my daughters was cut from the school volleyball team during try outs, and I'm kind of glad. I know you must be wondering how I could say such a thing. After all, it's hard to watch a kid experience the letdown of trying out for a team only to be told they are not good enough. Unfortunately, it's the hard lesson my daughter needed to learn. You see, that's what happens when you don't practice. Talent will only take you so far.

> One of my daughters was cut from the volleyball team, and I'm kind of glad.

I had warned my naturally athletic daughter for some time that she would need to practice more if she wanted to be one of the best at something. With only a week to go before tryouts, she spent only a few hours practicing on a couple different days.

Of course I wanted my daughter to make the team, but what would she have learned if she made the team with little to no practice? It was indeed a wakeup call.

Would you rather have your child have a wakeup call and learn a valuable lesson early in life or later in life? Are you winging it? Are they winging it? Do you practice good parenting? Do you practice more than you play? Do your children practice more than they play? I want my kids, and anyone else who wants to be the best at something, to acknowledge and accept the price that needs to be paid…the price of preparation.

A professional athlete, performer, or musician might practice 40 or 50 hours for every one hour that they're actually paid to play. Would you believe that Michael Jordan was cut from his high school basketball team his sophomore year? This drove him to practice more and to practice the right things more intently. Today he is still considered the greatest player of all time.

Highly accomplished individuals know that it's not just "practice makes perfect", but rather "perfect practice makes perfect". The details matter. What happens if we practice the wrong way? Yet, we as parents so many times just show up day after day hoping to figure it out on the fly. Why is that?

I suppose sometimes we have no choice. I suppose we are all balancing a lot of different things and sometimes practicing falls by the wayside. Wake up call! If you want to be really good at something, even parenting, you need to practice and be prepared.

Here are 7 activities that will better prepare you or your child for better "game time, show time" performance.

1. <u>Reading Books</u> – There are great books on almost every subject that will make you more knowledgeable. Reading this book is practice and preparation.

2. <u>Attending Seminars</u> – Hearing industry leaders speak on various topics and skill sets as you take notes can be a great way to learn more.

3. <u>Role Playing</u> – Yes, literally hearing objections from a "preparation partner" and practicing how to overcome those objections is paramount in parenting. You and your spouse can discuss and practice what you are going to say to your kids. If you are a single parent, find another parent that you can role play a little of what you want to say to your child and how they might respond.

4. <u>Creating Purposeful Presentations</u> – We all need our children to take action from time to time. Having clear, organized ways to express your solutions to various problems helps you come across in a way that will hold their attention. I know this sounds funny but have your facts ready, the challenge defined, and your solution worded right so you can sell your kids on your plan to improve things.

5. <u>Interview Successful Parents</u> – Finding out how other parents got to where they are can really help you avoid major pitfalls. Every kid and family is different, but there are a lot of creative ways to teach and inspire kids. I love seeing what other parents do.

6. <u>Have a Mentor</u> – Regularly talk with someone who is specifically at where you want to be. This is another way to avoid pitfalls and recognize big opportunities for breakthroughs. Not everyone has that mother, father, or family member they can reach out to, but you should have someone that you can talk to.

7. <u>Focus on Communication</u> – Make the art of listening, speaking to all walks of life, and perfecting accurate body language a constant pursuit. So much is determined by good or bad communication. Practice using different words and ways of saying things. Talk about things in front of a mirror, and watch your body language including smiles, hands, etc.

The stakes are high. Battles are won or lost by the level of preparation and practice. Many times, parents succeed or fail because of their level of preparation and practice. Do these seven activities regularly and you will put all the odds in your favor of being a highly successful Guerrilla Parent.

And, yes, I know this seems extreme and intense, but I am giving you the ways to put all the odds in your favor. Even if you added half of the beliefs and parenting techniques in this book to your life you would still have twice the parenting success.

Defining success is almost like defining love. There are a lot of different ways to do it and most of them aren't wrong. However some definitions of success seem to be more helpful to Guerrilla Parents than others. After all some truths have greater value, and this is the start of wisdom.

In order to better understand our definition of success you must understand that there's a long list of words that can be used during an intelligent conversation about the topic.

The success conversation may use words like hard work, discipline, perseverance, focus, drive, intelligence, good attitude, humility, confidence, systems, decision making, and patience. None of those would be wrong, but in defining the formula for success we want to say the least amount of words possible that will cover it all the most correctly.

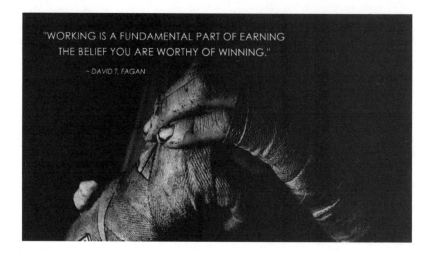

First, here is how most people define the formula for success:

Talent + Luck = Success

You see, a lot of the world explains away others' success as God-given talent or world-given luck. What this does is it takes the control and destiny out of their hands, implying that they are not able to reach success without some kind of higher power or outside factor.

This makes a lot of people feel better about where they are at in their lives so that they are not to blame. It makes them feel even better when someone who is more successful than they are can be explained away as well.

It's not uncommon to hear less successful people say certain things about more successful people like...

- Their family has money or they must come from money. If I came from money I would have more success too.

- They are attractive or good looking. If I was good looking I would have more success too.

- They are so lucky. If I was that lucky I would have more success too.
- They have so much more time than me. If I had more time like them I would have more success too.

And the list of excuses goes on. We need to take these excuses away from our children as well as ourselves. After all, they are watching you more than you know.

Now let me tell you what successful people know to be the formula for success:

Preparation + Opportunity = Success

People who practice, work hard, study, learn, role play, and perfect expertise are extremely prepared for whatever they come up against.

People who create options, manipulate their own luck, recognize chances, accurately assess risk, and easily project potential profits understand the power of opportunities.

WHAT MOST PEOPLE THINK CONSCIOUSLY OR SUBCONSCIOUSLY

$$Talent + Luck = Success$$

WHAT MOST SUCCESSFUL PEOPLE KNOW

$$Preparation + Opportunity = Success$$

WHAT REALLY SUPER SUCCESSFUL PEOPLE KNOW

$$\frac{Preparation^2 + Opportunity^2}{Wisdom} - Ego = Super\ Success$$

When these two are combined, few things are impossible. The more prepared you are, the bigger the opportunities you can take advantage of. Now if you really want to get scientific, more advanced, and be a student of super success then this is the formula you want:

Notice that there are two new major elements. The first is the addition of wisdom, which is the correct application of knowledge in all instances. Again, some truths just have more value than others.

Knowing when and how to apply knowledge is a lifelong pursuit. Every situation has multiple variables that involve perceptions, realities, people, and all different goals. Even now I am teaching Guerrilla Parenting, but in order for the teachings to be successful you will have to apply them to your children in varying, age appropriate ways because every kid and family is different.

To understand this and to be able to make Guerrilla Parenting decisions is to exhibit wisdom. We can't prepare for everything so we must choose carefully. We can't take on every opportunity so we must prune priorities based on whatever up-to-date information we have on hand.

We divide out from preparation and opportunities through our wisdom. The more wisdom, the better our choices and outcomes. We all know by now that every decision we have ever made has led us to right to where we are at in our lives. This will be the same for our children, so help them where you can.

The other major new element is the subtraction of ego. Few understand how dangerous pride can be. Now there are some exceptions, and this is where wisdom comes into play. Parenting pride can keep us from saying sorry when we are wrong, expressing love when our kids are difficult, and not showing love and tolerance for others in the world.

For example we need to have enough confidence to pursue our dreams. We need to believe in ourselves and what we are capable of.

That being said, our confidence and beliefs can cross over a line into egomania if we are not careful. Ego keeps us from asking questions, it makes us unteachable, and it refuses much needed help from others.

Many successful people become ego maniacs, but don't let this confuse you. Very few of them started out this way. Unfortunately ongoing success can make people believe that they are better than and greater than other people. Ego can make people forget what got them there in the first place.

Some parents actually compliment their kids so much they walk around saying "Aren't I so pretty?" and "I'm so smart." We must be careful to love and lead in the right way.

Of course, the little 2 by the word preparation and opportunity just means that these things are multiplied by each other for massive amounts of detail and completeness.

The super successful are often called obsessed, crazy, workaholics, and extreme. Of course the super successful are also called rainmakers, celebrities, and icons of industry. There can be a chip on their shoulder, a fire in their belly, and a burning in their brain.

Super success isn't for everyone and can mean different things for different people. Entrepreneurs typically feel like they are super successful when they have more money than time, the freedom to do what they want when they want, they get paid to do what they love, and they are celebrated by others as one of the best in their industry.

So how do you teach this to your kids? You must work with and beside them. Let them see you exercise, put in the long hours from time to time, do projects around the house, and go out in the community to serve. You teach by example.

Make sure you celebrate the completion of your work together whenever possible. Take time to stand back and look at that room you cleaned, the garage you organized, or that yard you trimmed. And if it doesn't look good, go back to work with your kid until it does so they know what it is like to work until the job is finished with a sense of satisfaction.

When your kids are first learning to work you must show them in real time, face to face, step by step. Next do it with them until they can do it without you. This is important. A Guerrilla Parent demonstrates how to do the task at hand, especially when their children are young.

It's good to have a reward when jobs are done, but sometimes we need to teach that a job well done is reward enough. Help them have a feeling of accomplishment through their work. Working hard is a lost art and a forgotten ethic.

Some of my favorite memories as a kid were working with my father on projects like building a deck. Now don't think for one second that I didn't do my fair share of whining or complaining, but I still learned to love to work. One of my greatest attributes in life that I owe most of my success to is the ability to work hard. I have always been able to learn and grow to make money because of my work ethic.

When parents give too much without having their kids work they teach the wrong lesson. Children think that they get things because that's what their parents are supposed to do. Kids grow to believe that their parents are supposed to give and that they are entitled to receiving. After all, they got things for nothing so why shouldn't they keep getting things for nothing, right? This is wrong!

Even the order in which work happens is important. By that I mean you work first and then you play. Doing it the other way promotes

> *T*each your kids to work first and then to play.

procrastination and develops habits that leave opportunities for important things to go undone.

Children can start by helping at a young age by running little errands inside of a home…

1. Throwing stuff away
2. Taking things from one room to another
3. Putting toys away
4. Setting things on a table
5. Taking things off a table

Eventually kids can…

1. Do dishes
2. Take out the garbage
3. Vacuum
4. Sweep
5. Mop
6. Clean rooms
7. Scrub toilets
8. Do laundry
9. And even cook

By the time my kids are ten they can make…

1. Eggs
2. Toast
3. Hot Cereal
4. French Toast
5. Sandwiches

By the time they are teenagers they can cook and bake…

1. Spaghetti
2. Fried Potatoes
3. Enchiladas
4. Cookies

5. Brownies
6. Cakes
7. Macaroni
8. Stir Fry
9. BBQ steak
10. BBQ chicken
11. BBQ salmon
12. French Toast
13. Pancakes

Working in the kitchen is a great way to spend time with kids. You learn how they think, process information, follow directions, and see their motor skills. Cooking is another lost art and a forgotten tradition that leaves some people less self-reliant, or at least limited in life to some measure.

All of these activities and more can help your kids learn a solid work ethic. I love to cook, thanks to my mom. I cook at least as much as my wife when I am in town. All my boys are learning to cook just like my daughters and they see my example.

First, spend time with your kids. Second, spend time working with your kids. And last, celebrate the time together and reward a job well done whenever you can. Guerrilla Parents put in the time.

Chapter 6
Attitude of Independence

Guerrilla Parents foster an attitude of independence. With nothing but safety of your child to hold you back, you should encourage your kids to take action, make things happen, and see things through. The down side to less independent children is that they need you all the time. What will happen if and when you can't be there for them? We must prepare them for this day sooner rather than later.

With nothing but safety to hold you back, encourage your child to take action.

I'm not talking about them having full time jobs at 5 or dating seriously by 6. I'm talking about having them do everything they can do safely by themselves for themselves. Here are some examples that may be too extreme for most parents:

1. We have a low cupboard with dishes in it. This cupboard is setup for kids as young as two to get stuff out to make a sandwich or get a bowl of cold cereal. There is a step stool nearby to get the milk out of the fridge or cereal out of the cupboard. They need to ask first if it's not a meal time, but otherwise they are encouraged to get what they need and not to wait for others. Yes, there is a mess that we are willing to help them clean up.

2. We teach our kids gun safety and to shoot guns as early as we can to reduce the odds of them getting hurt by a gun and to reduce their fear of weapons. Some have learned about guns as young as 5 years old, and all three of my teenage girls have gone shooting more than a few times.

3. We teach our kids to swim as early as possible to reduce the fear of water. We have almost always had a swimming pool or been around water. We don't want our kids to be afraid or to be unsafe.

4. We teach our older kids to take care of their younger brothers and sisters by looking out for them, entertaining them, and feeding them.

5. We teach our kids how to travel. We want them to be aware of what is going on around them, how hotels work, how airports work, how to take a bus, and even how to use trains and taxis. Eventually, they will use these things by themselves in pairs or even by themselves as early as 10 or 11.

6. I teach our kids to drive on private property first while sitting on my lap when they are 5 or 6 and then eventually by themselves at 12 or 13. It wasn't uncommon to have them learn to use the riding lawn mowers around 9 or 10 when we had acreage.

7. Most of our kids have started businesses at 7 or 8 doing lemonade stands, chores for neighbors, or even selling things they have made.

8. Our kids ask for things in public. I almost always have my kids order their own food from talking age on. They must learn to talk to people and communicate for what they want and need.

9. My kids know how to make their way around the neighborhood. They can go to the park, to a friend's,

or even walk to the school if it's close enough. Every neighborhood is different, but I want my kids to be able to get to places on their own whenever possible. They check in and follow up to let me know where they are.

10. All our kids learn to use technology. Although my kids don't have phones until roughly 11, they learn to use phones and computers pretty young so they can communicate safely.

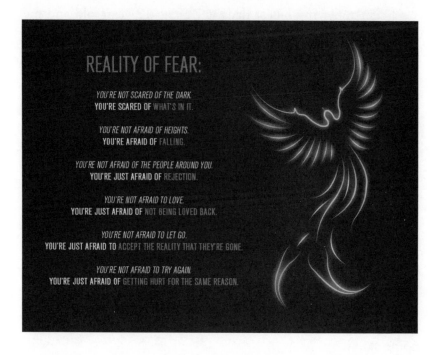

REALITY OF FEAR:

YOU'RE NOT SCARED OF THE DARK.
YOU'RE SCARED OF WHAT'S IN IT.

YOU'RE NOT AFRAID OF HEIGHTS.
YOU'RE AFRAID OF FALLING.

YOU'RE NOT AFRAID OF THE PEOPLE AROUND YOU.
YOU'RE JUST AFRAID OF REJECTION.

YOU'RE NOT AFRAID TO LOVE.
YOU'RE JUST AFRAID OF NOT BEING LOVED BACK.

YOU'RE NOT AFRAID TO LET GO.
YOU'RE JUST AFRAID TO ACCEPT THE REALITY THAT THEY'RE GONE.

YOU'RE NOT AFRAID TO TRY AGAIN.
YOU'RE JUST AFRAID OF GETTING HURT FOR THE SAME REASON.

I think most parents grew up in an era that was safer, or at least it seemed safer. This perceived safety, whether real or not, allowed us to wander and walk to places a little more frequently. I understand that times are different, but whenever we can and however we can we want are children to exercise independence.

Again, my personal family lifestyle is probably somewhat unique and more extreme than needed, but Guerrilla Parents should teach independence. Empower your kids to do age appropriate activities and maybe even push the envelope a little. At least give them the feeling of independence.

I check up and monitor my kids more than they probably realize for sure, but they are still learning and living as if they are making decisions on their own and taking care of themselves. This gives them the feeling of confidence they need to overcome fears, excelling in the area of independence, and taking calculated risks in life.

I remember my oldest daughter being 12 years old and me teaching her to drive in the empty, Mexican desert. Later that same week while on vacation I came across a van I wanted to buy in Mexico that was a really good deal. I couldn't drive back both our suburban and the van, so I had my daughter drive the suburban a couple miles back to our beach rental with me right in front of her. Needless to say, my wife was pretty upset when I showed up with two vehicles, my daughter Jordan driving one of them by herself. (I don't recommend this.)

There are some downsides to teaching your kids independence. One time, the police brought my 7 year old son home in a police car with his bike tied to the front. They said he had biked too far away and looked like he was by himself near a busy street. This is not something I had okayed. He was at a friend's house, and when the friend had to leave my son tried to follow him to the soccer field two miles away. While the cops said he had done nothing wrong, they just wanted to get him home safely.

I know this independent thing is starting to sound kind of bad, but it's real life. Let me share just one more story.

Not too long ago, I walked into my oldest daughter's room and looked at her whiteboard where she keeps all her ideas, schedules, bills, and goals. I noticed there was a $100 payment she had on the board as an ongoing bill.

When I asked her about it, she said she had kind of mentioned it before. I told her to mention it again. She explained that six months before she had accidently rear ended another driver and caused a very small amount of damage. She asked what she could do to make it right, so the driver got some estimates and gave her a bill she could pay off in monthly cash payments. She was still making payments and would for a while.

Of course, part of me thought she may have been taken advantage of or that what she agreed to pay was maybe too much or not necessary. Maybe she should have even let the insurance handle it. But mostly I was so pleased to see my daughter be able to maneuver a complicated discussion, negotiate out what she felt was right, and then continue to make payments all on her own.

This was the self-reliance and independence I always wanted for my children. More importantly I recognized her effort to do the right thing all on her own because of her sense of integrity. She not only made the deal but made the effort to pay it out all on her own. She didn't come to me expecting me to pay it off for her or to bail her out.

We can't have our kids living in fear, afraid to make mistakes. Danger is real and they need to understand risks, but fear is a self-reliance killer.

The contract on the next page is an adaptation of something I give to my coaching clients. Print this up and give it to your kids. Something magical happens when someone signs this or any contract.

When I travel, Sam is the man of the house. He has been the man of the house since he was 4 or 5 years old. Even his older sisters helped him to feel that way. He calls on someone to say family and dinner prayers, locks up the house at night, and helps tuck in younger kids with stories. The older he is, the more it means for him to be the man of the house. Now there are even times that his younger brother is the man of the house. It's so important that we give our kids something to live up to.

DAVID T. FAGAN'S
PERMISSION TO MAKE MISTAKES:

I _____ (the child), hereby acknowledge that on occasion it is completely normal, human, and expected for mistakes to occur. I pledge that when that happens I will not spend exorbitant amounts of time beating myself up over any setbacks or failures. I understand that I have full permission to make mistakes and am expected to make mistakes on a regular basis.

I am not afraid. I was born to do this.

Sign _____ Date_____

Here are some ways that any Guerrilla Parent can foster more independence and provide more real world views for their child:

1. Have your child try things first and get things started on their own whenever they can. The hardest is always the start. Having your kid try things on their own, even

if you are nearby, is a great thing to do. You might be surprised how well they do and how fast they realize they can do things on their own.

2. Look for things that you do for them that they can physically do for themselves. Things like getting dressed, picking out clothes, and tying shoes are safe things that kids can do on their own pretty quickly even if it isn't done entirely how you would do it for them. I once discovered I had a 10 year old that still couldn't tie their shoes. Needless to say, that became an immediate priority.

3. Teach them safety inside and what happens when people aren't safe. I'm always pointing out things in my home that are not safe. If a knife is left out, something left on the stairs, or dangerous things left in the reach of kids I point it out. Then I have a kid fix the problem as I watch. Remember, this is an attitude that starts with simple things.

4. Teach them safety outside and what happens when people aren't safe. How to cross a road, how far they can go on their own, and how long they can go places is important too.

5. Let your kids help with whatever needs to be done, even if it's holding something and standing nearby. There are lots of chores that you can do with your kids.

6. Help them raise money for whatever activities they want to do. It's okay to make up the difference from time to time when they fall short, but make sure they do their part for most things they get.

7. Have them watch you when you do things. Have a discussion about what you are doing and why you are doing it.

As your kids become teenagers or even close to teenagers then you need to…

1. Encourage them to speak up for their beliefs.
2. Ask friends to get together to do things after school.
3. Ask people out on dates.
4. Respectfully discuss with teachers things they don't understand or disagree with.
5. Stand up for others being treated unfairly.
6. Support them when they take risks.
7. Invest in any ways that will help them make money.
8. Help them understand costs, income, and profits.
9. Teach them the value of time and their time specifically.
10. Teach them the types of things people pay money for and what they pay the most for.

The more your kids understand these basics, the more prepared they are for the opportunities in life that will come.

I've done all these things and more, including making my kids try things they don't want to, like foods they didn't want to eat and sports they didn't want to play.

Independence comes from feeling unlimited. Feeling unlimited comes from overcoming limitations in whatever form you can.

I once made my 7 year old son play baseball. He was shy, and he didn't want people to stare at him. He didn't want to go to practice and pretty much cried off and on for the first couple weeks when it was time to get ready. But oh the feeling when he hit the ball in his first game. Oh what a feeling when he made friends on the team.

Since then I have made him try other sports as well, but he still says baseball is his favorite. Sometimes they need a push.

Don't forget, they really don't know what they want or need, let alone what they like.

BE YOUR
OWN HERO.
~UNKNOWN

I remember the first time one my daughters told me she loved to sing and wanted to sing more. I had heard her sing before and I was concerned because I thought she needed a lot more time to master this art. But I told her to practice like I always do. Before long she got into an advanced choir, was singing the national anthem at varsity games, and was doing it all on her own. She got better!

Sometimes we don't know what our kids are capable of or what they will be good at. On her own, she decided to try out for the TV show *The Voice* and went to stand in line for hours with thousands of others to audition. She actually got a call back, and even though that didn't go anywhere I was excited to see her find things she loved on her own and follow her dreams. As I write this she is now standing in line for another audition to another singing TV show.

Yes, there are risks that come from teaching your kids to be independent, but I think there are greater risks for not teaching them to be independent. You can start at any age but the younger the better.

Unlike the fairy tales we find in classic books, neither your daughters nor your sons should be waiting to be rescued.

Guerrilla Parents learn to inspire self-motivation and encourage risk taking. We also protect our kids' physical safety, but we teach what dangers are real and what fears are unsubstantiated. Guerrilla Parents must also overcome their own fears for their children. To reach their full potential, our children must be able to fall, fail, and learn on their own.

Chapter 7
Sharing the Good,
the Bad, and the Ugly

As parents we want to protect our kids on many levels. We want to shield them from life's hardness and the world's tough realities. Guerrilla Parents have tough conversations, share personal experiences, and discuss finances openly.

It wasn't long ago that a father confided in me that his family was having money troubles. He was so scared that his kids would find out. He didn't want them to worry or wonder about money. There was a lot of fear and uncertainty, and he believed his children were best off never knowing what was going on.

I will tell you now just like I told him then that this is wrong. Fathers and mothers should be willing and able to share some, if not most, of their financial situations. One of the most powerful words you can ever say to a child is "no". And even better is to explain why you can't buy them everything they want. They should know that you may not be able to do everything you want either.

So much is gained by your children seeing your struggle and your effort to organize the home finances. These are real things, real issues that kids need to experience and understand how ever they possibly can.

By doing this they can become more sensitive to how money is spent, what things cost, and that money does not grow on trees. Yes, I know many parents tell their kids that money doesn't grow on trees, but how many really explain it with a little more detail consistently throughout a year.

I'm not saying you need to tell your 5 year old that they may not have a home to live in or a bed to sleep in if things go wrong. I am just saying that you should share some of the real finances.

> **Share some of the real finances of your home.**

You don't need to know exactly what you are worth or how much you have saved, but you should share roughly what you make and what budgets you have.

These discussions prepare them for what it takes to make a living and provide for themselves. These conversations may be very generalized when kids are younger, but by the time they are 8 to 10, things should get more specific. By the time they are teenagers they should have a pretty clear understanding of what it takes to pay for your style of living as well as what it would take for you to have a higher or lower cost of living.

Things to share with your kids through various ages are...

1. How much you pay for where you live.
2. How much you pay for transportation, including insurance and gas if applicable.
3. How much food costs in your home.
4. What utilities run.
5. How much you spend in general on vacations, holidays, and birthdays.
6. How much you save and why.
7. How much you make gross and net.
8. How much you might pay in taxes and why (good luck on that one).
9. How much the family spends on fun and entertainment.
10. How much the family spends on clothes and gear.

11. How much the family spends playing sports, music, and other extra-curricular activities.
12. How much you invest and why.

I once showed my kids some of the things we consume, use, or do as a family of 10 every month on average.

- 29 gallons of milk
- 156 eggs
- 33 loaves of bread
- 90 oz of Peanut Butter
- 96 oz of Jam/Jelly
- 32 rolls of toilet paper
- 67 pounds of meat
- 33 pounds of potatoes
- 48 peppers
- 22 onions
- 65 pounds of fruit
- 7500 text messages
- 251 gallons of gas

Because of how we value our time, we typically have a groundskeeper, pool man, and for close to a decade we had a full time house manager. Sometimes the house manager has lived with us and sometimes they have not, but they still average working 40 hours a week.

It's made very clear to our kids that these people are here for us and work for us. They are not around to make my kids' lives easier, to clean their rooms, or do their chores.

Delegation is a concept deeply explained and encouraged. Once my older kids start making money it's not unusual for them to pay their younger siblings to do their chores around the house. We very much run our house like a business. Even our dining table is really a conference room table.

Kids always benefit from object lessons and visual activities. One of the best things you can do to teach them about money is to pay them for jobs in cash. (If they have ways to make money outside the home then make sure that money gets turned into cash as well.) Then give them different zip lock bags or zipper pouches to put the money into.

It's not unusual for older kids to pay younger siblings to do their chores.

Be prepared with plenty of change and smaller bills so they can split up the money easily. This allows them to continually divide up their money, which they love by the way, into very specific categories. Clear bags are great because they can see the money inside. Coins are okay too because they love to feel the weight and hear the jingle. Funny, I know, but true.

The conventional and most common thing taught is to take your kid down to the bank to open a savings account, but this comes much later and is less important in the grand scheme of things.

Now we'll talk about the categories. Keep in mind that your child needs to have all of these bags, and they have to use the money in the way it's intended.

First, have a bag for tithing or charity so that they learn to give back. Have two bags for savings – one for short term purchase goals like a bike or a toy and one for long term goals like college or a car. They need a bag for fun and entertainment for things like movies or books. You might ask why they are required to spend some on fun things, but this is crucial to helping them learn that life is to be enjoyed. They need to work hard and then enjoy the fruits of their labors. The last bag is for taxes that, in this case, go to the home...so to speak. This may also be a strange concept, but kids need to know the realities of life. They aren't going to be able to escape taxes in the real world and should learn this as soon as they start earning money. It helps them appreciate it more.

The money should be split like this.

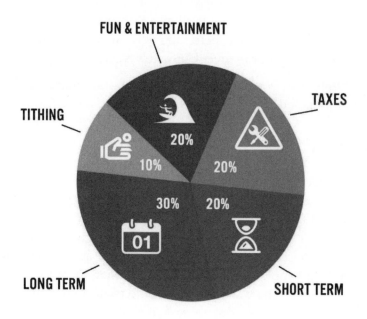

<u>Tithing and Charity</u>

I think it's important to teach kids to give back and share their blessings. We pay tithing, but we also support causes we believe in through charities. Sometimes kids will be more motivated by helping others than even by getting things for themselves. Being socially conscious and learning to give out of free will is important. In our home, 10% is almost mandatory although we have never had a kid fight us on this before. If done right, you will have tough decisions to make when your child wants to give even more than you ask.

For me this conversation goes something like this. "A farmer needs to have enough money to live to see another day and enough money to buy seeds to plant and grow more crops. If the farmer doesn't eat, have a place to sleep, have seeds to plant, and tools to do the planting, then they can't grow the crops that later they want to sell for a profit or to share with those that need it most. We can't give it all away or even too much of it away. There is a balance here, and I want to give you some options on how you can give. Ultimately, you get to decide."

Obviously, you can build out or elaborate more on these types of metaphors and analogies.

Savings

Decide on some short term and long term goals. These goals can even change a little, especially when it comes to short term goals. Once kids have to work for things they might change their mind on what is really valuable to them and what isn't. It's interesting to see kids have toys that break and watch their reaction to the money they spent, the time they spent saving the money, and even the work they had to do to make the money in the first place all to get something that broke.

Their reaction may vary based on how the toy broke, too. If it broke because it wasn't made very well that's a good conversation and life lesson about how you spend your money on buying quality made items. If it broke because they misused it or didn't care for it then that's a good conversation and life lesson about how to treat things we own. Either way, the lessons are almost most endless and totally priceless.

Fun and Entertainment

The money saved for fun and entertainment is mostly for when kids want to go do things with other kids. If we are doing something as a family, then I don't require them to pay of those things. I might take my family out to eat, to the movies, to do some school shopping, or even on a family trip. I cover these costs. Maybe they want a special treat I don't want to buy for them or maybe they want some kind of technology that I don't want to buy for them. Either way, these are just more examples of how they might want spend their fun and entertainment money.

Taxes

Now taxes are a tricky one but an important one. If they spend their money wisely, then I will give them all their money back. See, I'm much nicer than the government. You can use their tax money to give back to them for business development, non-profits they want to support, something we want to do together as a family, or even money they want to lend out to other family members. All in the name of having fun and stimulating the family economy. After all, more well off kids in the home may delegate and hire other kids in the home.

We don't always use the cash and bag system because it takes a lot of time and monitoring. We'll do it for a few months and then take a break before we start it up again. But even just a few months of this process is good. As time goes on they will do a certain percentage of these things on their own, which is really what you are working towards. You shouldn't have to monitor and make sure money is spent the right way all the time. The idea here is to teach them well and then to let them govern themselves as much as possible.

My older kids are always paying tithing and saving for various things without me ever really asking or monitoring. My kids are regularly making money and using their money for the things they know I won't buy. The activity is just to get momentum and teach some important money concepts.

Here are some more money activities to do with your kids to get them thinking in the terms of family and individual time, money, and lifestyle.

Money Activity #1

Don't be proud or ashamed to share these numbers. It should be discussed almost clinically to better prepare your kids for what the real world looks like. Get them asking questions. Ask them if they would do anything different. If they want something, ask them how you would do that based on your budget or income.

Money Activity #2

Don't lead them; rather, let them design the kind of life they want to live someday and then match up the associated costs with their dream lifestyle. Help them understand what it will take and then show them the types of businesses or jobs that will make that kind of money. Then show them the types of education they would need to live that kind of life.

Money Activity #3

Discuss credit. Explain how credit works with scores from records of paying bills on time. Share how banks will extend lines of credit or provide money for things that you must then pay back plus interest. Explain the risks, the fees, and the extra money paid for interest. You may even want to and need to lend them money when they do businesses. Even if they do a lemonade stand, they need to know that the things they are using to make money cost something to start with.

Many times I have shared with my kids when people owe me money, when I owe people money, when we had a good month or a bad month, and what our business plans are to increase profits or have more time in our life.

These money conversations are priceless and should happen almost regularly. Your kids should have a very real idea of what things costs including homes, cars, and food.

Don't get me wrong: life is not all about making money. I don't care what my kids make in terms of money as long as they can have a good life being self-reliant. Some might say that they can only have a good life if they make good money, but those people are wrong.

I think happy, successful people can be summed up in two ways.

1. They work to play. These people have a business or most likely a job that they do so they have money to enjoy the hobbies they love which is where they get their real joy. Their business or job is just a means to an end. These people are not fulfilled by what they do to make money. They are more fulfilled by what happens outside of their work.

2. Work is play. These people are defined by their careers or business. They get as much joy working as they do anything else, if not more. They are excited to work and are passionate about reaching new levels in their

industry. They have hobbies, but their biggest love is their work.

Neither one of these lifestyles are wrong. One person might even spend time in both areas over the course of their life.

I think unhappy, unfulfilled people can be summed up in two other ways.

1. They hate work. They don't have the education, skill set, or mind set to break free into something better so they live a lot of their lives sick and tired. They are a slave to their work and are burnt out pretty quickly. They may even quit or live in very poor conditions.
2. They have an unhealthy relationship with work. They work too much, sacrifice too much, and live life out of balance. They typically end up alone and with regrets.

Obviously we want to help our kids avoid these unhappy situations which are very real possibilities. Many people think that I am terrible because I won't pay for things for my kids. This just isn't true. As a matter of fact, I think parents always pay one way or another.

You can invest in your kids when they are young, teaching them self-reliance and providing them with opportunities to make money or you can pay for them later in life when they can't support themselves. You can pay now in certain ways or you can pay later in certain ways. Either way you are going to pay. Guaranteed.

Guerrilla Parents invest in developing in their kids' talents, getting them supplies for their own businesses, teaching them about real life and real costs, and showing them ways to create profits. Guerrilla Parents value schooling but look to customize education whenever possible.

This is an attitude of sharing real life that many want to shield their kids from or even hide from themselves. I don't believe in making my kids have an easy life or even an easy time. I don't even let them win at games.

I will try to play somewhat at a kid's level, but in the end I am going to try to win within reason. I am going to make it hard for my kids to beat me at Scrabble, Risk, Monopoly, or even Settlers. It takes years for my kids to beat me if they ever do at all, but when they win you would think they had won the gold medal at the Olympics.

Some of my kids are more competitive than others, but they all are good at games and want to win. Winning is an attitude at our home. They learn how to be a good winner as well as a good loser. This is another lost art in the world today.

Now we live in a world of no-keeping-score sports, multiple valedictorians, everyone gets a certificate, and downplaying who the best is. This is wrong. We learn a lot from losing, and that's real life.

You won't always win. And when you don't it's in that moment that you create your deepest convictions that you never want to lose again. Harnessing heartbreak empowers you to change your future forever.

Guerrilla Parents are tough love people. They know that they are doing their kids no favors by letting them win, making life extra easy, and shielding them from losses. Guerrilla Parents share and experience the good, the bad, and the ugly for their kids' benefit.

Chapter 8
School

I've always loved Mark Twain's quote, "Never let school get in the way of your education." The good news is that there is a growing amount of options nowadays when it comes to schools and education. Just remember, the focus is always education, not necessarily schools.

Ultimately it's your responsibility to worry about your children as individuals and ultimately it's the school's job to worry about classes. See the problem?

So if your kid fits into the system with a certain kind of personality and has an average style of learning you will be in pretty good shape. Of course, if your child has any kind of learning disability or if your child is exceptionally bright your child may be limited or underserved.

This is rarely a teacher or administration problem. Like I said before, I believe most people in the school to be good hearted individuals full of good intentions. Unfortunately, many times they are overworked, underpaid, and rarely compensated for the right things.

Just remember schools, public schools especially, are not equipped to really help most kids as individuals and they are working with outdated information and systems.

> *Most* public schools are not equipped to help kids as individuals.

Here are just a few things I have personally experienced that are just wrong:

1. A kindergartner getting homework even on weekends.
2. A math teacher that doesn't speak English very well because it's their second language.
3. Cramming classes into a statewide schedule for Common Core, which doesn't allow much time for kids who don't understand concepts.
4. Making kids learn to write in cursive so they can read it if they happen upon it later in life.
5. A teacher spending class periods talking about her exploits in Mexico instead of teaching the Spanish language.

I kept the list short on purpose because this isn't about beating up on our school systems. Some might say homeschooling is the answer, and maybe it is for some kids. Some parents have the time and the skill set to educate their kids.

As long as these homeschool kids are getting opportunities to socialize elsewhere through sports, music, and other extra-curricular activities then I think this is okay. We have home schooled some of our kids here and there, but for the most part we have always used the public schools.

I was able to take two of my daughters out of school at different times for a semester here or there to provide them with opportunities to come work with me, travel with me, and go through intern programs that are typically only designed for college students.

I recognize that these are not opportunities that all parents can provide, but it just proves to me that so much of what is taught in school is a waste of brain power that helps no one. I agree that sometimes we just need to learn certain things and do certain things to prove that we can do hard things, but there is way too much teaching of worthless topics.

Others parents focus on private schools, but most people can't afford these options. Even then private schools are all about getting your kids into the best colleges, and I just don't believe every kid is meant to go to college.

Before a parent spends $30,000 to $60,000 a year for private school or college they could spend much less to help their child better understand who they are and what they want to do. You could spend $1,000 to $5,000 (or even less) to help your kid start a business. Two magical things can happen here.

One, they do well and they now have options. Or two, they don't do well and everyone gains a greater appreciation for the need for more formal schooling.

Schooling should really be customized. The concept of electives is going in the right direction, but doesn't go far enough. Teenagers should be given more opportunities to learn about real job options and how to run their own business.

> *S*chooling must be customized.

I think we forget that colleges these days are really businesses that make money. I am all about capitalism and love to see businesses succeed. That being said, we should know what they are selling, what everyone is buying, and ask if the ends justify the means for each child individually.

Here are 7 unconventional things to consider when raising and educating an entrepreneur:

1. Don't be afraid to hold back a kid who isn't doing well. We did this once and it was the best thing for the child at the time. Education is not a race to the finish line.
2. Don't be afraid to pull your kid out of school and try something different if things are not working. See what your area has to offer in the way of other education options.

3. If your kid has social problems, don't take them out of school or social situations just to make it easier. This child needs some kind of school more than anyone else.

4. Look for summer camps that can help your kid develop new talents and give you insight into what opportunities your child will benefit from most.

5. Look for sports, music, and other extra-curricular activities in which your child can try to develop their talents.

6. Be careful not to overload your child's schedule with non-stop activities. Three or four days a week, or five to six hours a week, of activities is plenty more than enough for most kids. Teenagers can do more, and you might find that this is good for keeping them out of trouble.

7. Help your kids make money to travel, try new things, and discover culture through restaurants, plays, concerts, and museums.

The overall idea here is that because you can't count on schools you need to do more. Guerrilla Parents do more. They spend time with their kids. They get to know their kids. They make the tough decisions when they have to, even if it is unconventional.

One of my kids wasn't taking school seriously and was hanging around some bad influences. I pulled the child out and had them come to work with me or do school from home. I gave them time and attention with a focus on business studies that challenged them in new ways.

It was an extreme move for an extreme situation. There was a lot of love given, a lot of options shared about money making possibilities, confidence was increased, and this child went back to school a year later never really missing a beat. We were both better for it.

On the other hand, I have another child that is a straight A student athlete that lives for and thrives in school. They worry about being on time, getting their homework done and getting good grades without me or my wife ever really getting involved. This child knows they need to get scholarships to go to college and are working hard to make it all happen.

Every child is different so not every school situation is going to be the same. Guerrilla Parents are prepared to know each child individually and find out what they need to excel at life.

Chapter 9
Technology

The innovations of the internet, phones, and computers have changed the way people can make money. It has also improved the way we can raise a self-reliant kid into an adult.

> *Technology is a sword that cuts both ways.*

Of course, technology is one of those swords that cut both ways. It can hurt as much as help if not careful. Some parents decide to avoid most of the internet when it comes to their kids altogether.

Keep in mind that technology is its own language. One of the few advantages a young person has more naturally is that they are on the cutting edge of the newest things online just through our culture. Safety comes first, but make sure your kids have access to technology.

It was young people between the ages of 15 and 25 that made Facebook take off...and now it's occupied primarily by 35 to 55 year olds. It was young people that set that trend. Something similar happened with MySpace, Twitter, YouTube, and now most have moved to Instagram.

When I have my kids work with me or for me, the top things I training them on and use them for are computer related. Young people almost instantly understand IM Chat, Social Media, Database Management software, Project Management Software, and Website creation and monitoring tools.

One of my teenagers' more sophisticated businesses is their

virtual assistant company, www.HireaTeenToday.com. The VA world has mostly gone overseas, but there is almost nothing that foreign workers can do that your teen couldn't with little training. These are valuable skills that can be easily honed and even more easily marketed. Plus, they never even have to leave home to work at some minimum wage job in the fast food world.

Here are some of the best programs for your kids, and especially teenagers, to learn:

Contact Management Systems that track emails, digital campaigns, contact records, online contact activity, and web form activity. Some of these systems include…

1. Infusionsoft
2. AWebber
3. 1Shopping Cart
4. Office Auto Pilot
5. Constant Contact

Project Management tools that companies use to track clients, multi-step check lists, and update multiple players and departments. This might include…

1. Basecamp
2. Wrike
3. Technopedia

Social Media is how a lot of companies are managing and growing their social public relations. They use them to advertise, recruit employees, and find new clients. They include…

1. LinkedIn
2. Twitter
3. Facebook
4. Instagram
5. YouTube
6. Pinterest
7. Tumblr

Other programs like WordPress to build websites, Zopim to hook IM Chat on the site, Power Point to build presentations, software to transcribe dictation, phone systems to set up conference calls, GotoWebinar to setup and host webinars, and Final Cut to record and edit audio and video can all be huge assets to an entrepreneur.

None of these programs are typically hard or as time consuming as most college courses. These are all very marketable skills that can pay a fair wage working from home.

I strongly discourage kids from being connected through the internet on their own in their bedrooms. I believe computers and phones that can be connected to the internet need to be in public places with vigilant monitoring.

We have a good filter on our internet but even then I try to collect all phones every night. This discourages texting, sexting, bullying, and all kinds of other problems that are all too prevalent these days.

> *There are risks we should prepare our kids to face, not avoid.*

Still there are a lot of risks out there in the world. I believe we need to prepare for them, not avoid them altogether. Your kids will need technology to become self-reliant.

Here is a more complete list of ways to keep your kids safe online:

1. Have access to all your kids accounts on their phone and online so you can check in on them from time to time.
2. Have a good internet filter. We use the internal filter on our router as well as other programs on each computer.
3. Keep technology in public areas.
4. Collect phones and any other portable, online devices every night.

5. Explain to kids the dangers. Even having an occasional family meeting to share updates is important.
6. Whenever possible have your kids use the buddy system when online.

Guerrilla Parents keep their kids safe and give them the weapon of technology to further ensure a life self-reliance. You must know the path of growth, new job markets emerging, and be able to think unconventionally so you can even work from home if you want or need to.

Chapter 10
Communication

This isn't a very exciting word or sexy topic, but communication really is fundamental in Guerrilla Parenting. You can't teach, inspire, and help your child develop their talents without good communication.

Listening, choice of words, language patterns, timing, and body language are all crucial when communicating a message with kids.

At the risk of assuming too much, I am not going to spend too much time on basic verbal and non-verbal communication skills. I am going to focus more on what I call Expression Rituals. These are longer activities that involve a deeper, more diverse combination of movements, words, and actions that are done in an ongoing, timely way.

The purpose of these Expression Rituals is to increase bonds of love, levels of trust, and degrees of confidence which is the foundation of a child with inner strength.

Your children will need to try new things, step outside of their comfort zone, work through criticism from others, keep working at things that don't come easy, and overcome fears. All these things are more easily accomplished when a kid has self-worth, knowing they have talents, intelligence, and someone cheering them on.

Expression Rituals can communicate a lot of feelings all at once. They have the ability to anchor feelings and ideas so that your child won't forget what you make matter most.

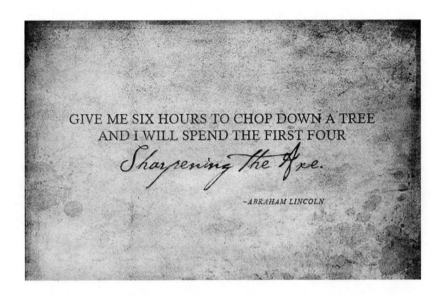

GIVE ME SIX HOURS TO CHOP DOWN A TREE
AND I WILL SPEND THE FIRST FOUR
Sharpening the Axe.

~ABRAHAM LINCOLN

Some of these ER's are more obvious traditions that can be done annually. For example:

1. <u>Breakfast in bed for birthdays</u> – Jill had this tradition growing up and I was notified by her family that it was my job to keep it going. Every child gets to pick their breakfast, we all go into their room, sing to them and give them their breakfast. Simple but powerful.

2. <u>Their Birth Story</u> – Jill tells each child about their birth and the day they were born on their birthday. Kids love stories, especially stories that have them in it.

Other ER's are more sporadic, although more common over the course of a month. For example:

1. <u>Trips to the store</u> – I never make a trip to the store by myself if at all possible. I always try to take one kid with me. It's our time together – just the two of us. I can focus on them, what's going on in their life, and work together to run an errand. If the kids are younger then it's more about holding their hand, pushing them in the cart, or letting them pick something out. If they are

older it's more about talking to them about school and their friends.

2. <u>Playing Catch</u> – Throwing a ball back and forth is fun for boys and girls of almost all ages. If they are young then it's kicking the ball back and forth. It's exercise, coordination, and maybe even laughing. I love these moments and wish I could do them more. Some of my best memories are throwing the Frisbee as a family, playing family football, competitive soccer, volleyball and even family badminton.

3. <u>Reading Stories</u> – Kids love stories. Time together spent reading is huge. Watching their wheels turn as you read the story is priceless. Sometimes stopping to ask questions, engage them in the story, or even changing something up to see if they are listening can be very revealing of your child's talents.

4. <u>Making Up Stories</u> – My kids love my made up stories more than anything. They are disappointed if I read instead of make one up. I usually use their names in the story, create funny or outrageous situations, and combine elements from other stories that they have already heard before. One of my favorite things to do is to start a story and then give them an option. Do you want the story to take place in the ocean or the sky? I might give them an option about a character. Do you want the hero to climb the tree or go into the cave? Pretty soon I have them creating the story without even knowing it. A lot can be learned about a kid through this exercise.

5. <u>Long Hugs</u> – My teenage girls seem to benefit from long hugs, even if they refuse a little in the beginning. This isn't always easy for me either because teens can be so difficult. (As a matter of fact, several of the things in this list can be hard for a parent. They take time, for us to come out of our comfort zone and for us to do some things that maybe don't come easy.)

Conversations go better. There is more listening and love with some hugs in and around the discussions.

6. <u>Take an interest in what your kids like</u> – This isn't always easy either, but I try to ask about my kids' video games and the TV shows they like. I try to watch them and be interested as they play. Most of the time it's not that hard to do.

7. <u>Wrestle time</u> – This may not always work depending on the ages, boys vs girls, and moms vs. dads but I like to wrestle with my boys. They all pile on. I try to play with them and rough them up in an age appropriate way. Physical contact, playing rough, and wrestling around can show kids that they can get a little hurt and still be okay. This may sound funny, but a lot of kids really don't know what to expect with physical contact. They are scared of sports, competition, and don't know how to act in various situations.

8. <u>Watching sports together</u> – Having a team, discussing rules, sharing insights, and talking about the story lines of the players can be very rewarding. There are lots of opportunities to share teaching moments, what a kid can learn from hard work, practice, and being a good sport. Raising a good sport, a fan, and someone who appreciates and looks up to talent in the right ways is important. These conversations can lead to them wanting to try various sports.

9. <u>Cooking in the Kitchen</u> – We already discussed this a little, but as a recap it's great to pass down recipes and work together in a kitchen environment. Plus they can see the result of their efforts pretty quickly when they get to try the food. So many great conversations and comparisons can be had and made in the kitchen together. You can learn a lot about your child as they follow the directions, estimate, and handle ingredients.

10. <u>Board Games and Puzzles</u> – Another chance to teach what it means to be a good sport, rules of engagements,

strategy, and luck. These are all very useful life skills. There should be fun, laughter, and it's okay for things to get a little intense. That's also real life. I know there have been some tears in my home doing a game or two.

All of these things involve you spending time with your child in various situations. They are scenarios that offer seemingly small opportunities to teach patience, love, and give honest compliments as they come naturally.

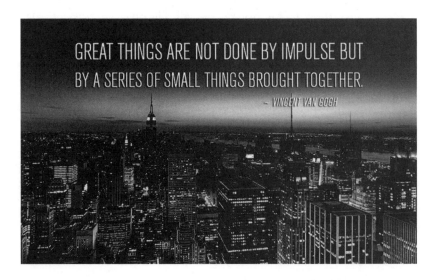

GREAT THINGS ARE NOT DONE BY IMPULSE BUT BY A SERIES OF SMALL THINGS BROUGHT TOGETHER.

~ VINCENT VAN GOGH

These moments will stay with a kid. They give the child skills that they can use one on one with friends, in a classroom, or on a team. When kids miss out on these opportunities it's left up to the schools and coaches to teach these lessons, which is never quite the same. A kid needs a parent as well as a teacher, mentor, and coach to help them excel with confidence and self-reliance.

If you do these things right, then you are already making eye contact, having good body language, and listening. You can't do these Expression Rituals without good communication. That's why I push the ER's over the fundamentals of communication.

If Expression Rituals are one powerful strategy to communicate, then the second powerful strategy to communicate is to use Perspective Pairing Questions. These are questions that allow you to learn a lot about a topic from the perspective of your child. Understand that this is not about reality and true facts, rather it's insight into the way your child thinks, feels, and believes.

These questions come in twos. The first question is designed to get something very specific. The second question is a follow up to the first question that is designed to find out how they perceive that experience, idea, or activity.

I call the first question a Specific Question and the second question a Feeling/Thinking/Believing question or FTB for short.

For example:

Specific Question – "Who did you play with at recess today?" (The only response can be names or no one.)

FTB Question – "How did you like it?" (There are many responses possible here. Don't be surprised if the answer is that they don't know.)

This is a process and you will have to keep with. Sometimes I feel like turning to a judge and asking for permission to treat the kid as a hostile witness because I can't get what I want.

Other Specific Questions might be...

1. Where did you go today?
2. Who were you with?
3. Who are your friends?
4. What did your teacher say?
5. What did your coach say?
6. What grade did you get?
7. Did you study?
8. Did you practice?

9. Do you like…?
10. Do you enjoy…?

These Specific Questions can be followed up by FTB Questions like…

1. How much fun did you have?
2. What do you believe?
3. Do you agree?
4. Do you see where they are coming from?
5. What would you do differently next time?
6. What do you like better?
7. What would you rather do?
8. Did you learn anything?
9. Why do you think you did that?
10. Why do you think that happened?

Remember, the idea here is to just get your kids talking, sharing, and communicating with you. Most of the time, the questions and answers are not as important as you learning about your child's perspective, their world, and their life.

There are many communication techniques and styles. Some kids that have encountered abuse or have been diagnosed with various learning disabilities may need more or different techniques.

Bottom line, Guerrilla Parents find creative ways to get their child communicating, and they are learning how to better serve them. Guerrilla Parents want to help their kids grow and reach their full potential.

Chapter 11
Entrepreneur Attitude

Raising an entrepreneur means creating a certain kind of lifestyle and attitude in your home. This is a cultural all its own and it's even a religion since one definition of religion is a way of life.

It's a way of living, week in and week out, month in and month out. It may not be an everyday kind of thing but it's a series of observations, conversations, activities, and business experimenting.

Here is one basic conversation to have with your child in an age appropriate way, meaning you may expound on these concepts more or less depending on their age or excitement for entrepreneurial activities.

This is something I teach adult business owners all the time in seminars and conferences. I call it Zero to Hero. How you go from Zero to Hero is as easy as 1-2-3. First comes Learning, then Earning, and finally Investing. Just look at the following diagram.

We need to develop talents, learn skill sets, and provide the best products or services we can. Next we can earn money, earn credit and even earn venture capital from investors. We need to save and make more that we owe. This can be done by keeping our costs low. When we make more than we owe, we want to reinvest back into ourselves and our business as well as our financial freedom someday.

Now look at the next diagram. Pretty similar except that this one is in an infinity symbol representing that this is a never ending process.

This is how I have built my businesses more than once. I have also lost it all and had to start over. Still this is a good way to start to understand entrepreneurialism going from zero to hero.

Help your kids know where they are at in the process at all times.

This diagram is to get kids thinking about doing what they love.

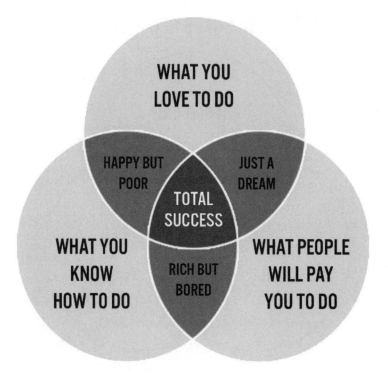

This should help kids figure out how to get the most out of their lives. Just look at the questions. Even though this may not be accurate for young kids, it's still good to know what you are shooting for. This thought process helps form good, recurring conversations.

Next I want to talk about goals. Goals are good, but I'm not much for long term goals. I think is messes people up by delaying action, thinking too long term, and getting people to lock into long term decisions based on the little knowledge they currently have.

Still, you want to make goals with your kids typically in 90 day settings. I call these Power Plays. It's something you can do right away in a short amount of time that will get you positive results. Check out the Venn Diagram on Goals.

We want adults and kids alike to fail forward fast, learn from mistakes, and find success through brilliant decision making.

"I either win or I learn."

- John Maxwell

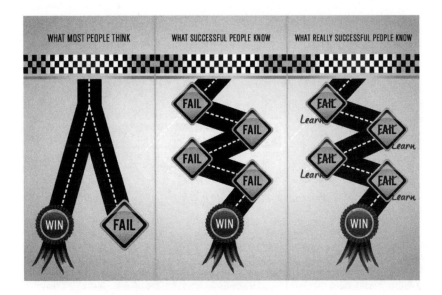

You see, these are the kinds of things they really don't teach in school. These are the kinds of perspectives and thought patterns that change the way young people view the world. There are more possibilities when you start to learn these kinds of business concepts I created for entrepreneurs in the real world every day.

I find that most kids, and especially teenagers, have no problem understanding what I am telling them. The visual aids help as well. You can download all these diagrams and images at our website, www.GuerrillaParenting.com/teachingtools.

You have to teach your child that if they are not willing to learn, no one can help them, but if they are determined to learn, no one can stop them!

And you can't let them worry too much about what they can't change. Sure, we want them to care, but worry doesn't help so here is another visual aid.

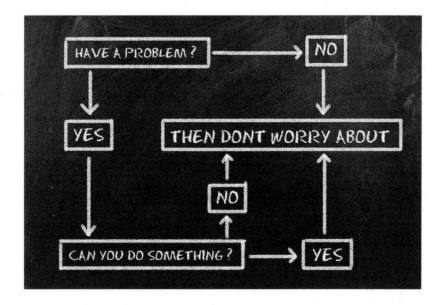

We want conversations about ways to make money, ways to enjoy life, and goals we have in the short term future that will provide opportunities for the long term future.

Here are some other great entrepreneur activities:

When you see an empty building for rent, ask your child what business would do well in that location. Point out what other businesses are nearby and if there are a lot of other empty spaces around the area. See if you can notice what kind of traffic the front of the store gets and if people can see the front door from the street driving by. Pretty soon your child can be recognizing opportunities and become more aware of the role real estate can play in a business.

Get on Craigslist with your child and check the FREE section to see what people are giving away. Then appraise the value of it by looking to see what people are selling the item for elsewhere on Craigslist online. See if you can figure out why they are getting rid of the item. Even have your kid call and talk to the owner. Get your kid involved in the process. Let them pick items that they know about or care about. Pretend that you're going to get it and discuss how would you pick it up, store it, advertise it, and eventually sell it. Just the thought process alone is priceless and very revealing.

1. Pick an industry and talk about how that industry makes money. For example, social media platforms are free so they make money through advertisers. Theatres don't make money through ticket sales so they make their money at concession stands. Discuss why stores so commonly will have items that they sell below market value to get people into stores.

2. Watch for ads and commercials to discuss. You can google Super Bowl commercials and find a whole bunch of them in one place. Watch a dozen or so and ask which ones they like, why they like them, and if you think the ad actually helps the business and how. Maybe they are funny, memorable, or make a good point. Have them think about how much money the company might spend and if they are going to make a profit on the commercial. This is called an ROI, or return on investment.

Let's talk about advertising more and the difference between big business advertising and small business advertising. Your kids need to know this because they should have ways to make money that will require some basic advertising or some level of guerrilla marketing.

Big businesses can afford to broadcast big ads on big stations talking to the general public. Small business owners typically need to nanocast more targeted ads to their specific audiences. This will give a small business owner a better ROI. In other words, big businesses can advertise just for the sake of advertising and brand management. Small business owners, on the other hand, need more results from their ads and can't afford to just get their name out there for the sake of having their name out there.

For example, a teenager that makes money babysitting would have to pay tens of thousands of dollars to broadcast an ad on television. Most of the people that heard the ad wouldn't even need that service. That same teen could also go pass out a flyer to parents at a church nursery for practically nothing and find a few new clients. This is the perfect cheap and easy message to market match. We know that the nursery is filled with young kids that have parents and our only cost is to create a flyer.

Now here is what makes a good ad for a small business owner, which is what 99% of all kids are going to be.

1. Get Attention – You must get the attention of the prospective buyer or clients. This means using images, words, and colors that stand out. This means putting your ad or message in a strategic place at a strategic time. If you can't get any attention, the rest of the ad is pointless.

2. Intriguing, Fascinating, Memorable message – You must create a solution to a problem in the shortest, most powerful way possible. Using alliterations, a play on words, and maybe even a rhyme can help an ad break through the static in the world all around us. Something that is clever and not easy to forget is always good. The ad must get some people to feel like you are talking to them. You can start the ad strong getting their attention, but if you don't provide a clear solution the prospect has no real reason to care.

3. Call to Action – The ad should always end with what you want the prospect to do like calling, texting, emailing, private messaging through social media, opting in on a website, or even going to a physical location. The call to action should be compelling and have a high perceived value. You can create the best ad

in the world, but if they don't know what you want them to do next the ad has failed.

When your kids have money this is a good checklist to use. You can also use these advertising basics as a way have discussions about other ads. Look out for billboards you like, signs that standout, and even the ads that you don't like. Pretty soon your kids will be noticing ads and marketing all around them forming opinions on what they like, don't like, and why. It's pretty cool to see your kids understand marketing and advertising.

Your kids will also benefit from some basic sales training. The crazy cool fact of the matter is that the younger the kid the more easily impressed adults will be by any sales process at all. Even if the adult seems upset it's probably just because they hate to say no to a kid. Typically the older and less cute a kid gets over time the more it can hurt their natural ability to sell. By the time they are older teenagers and adults they have to have more real world sales abilities to really get major results.

The bottom line is that we need to teach our kids how to handle a "no". Not just for the sake of making sales but so that they can learn how to handle rejection as well. Life has lots of rejection, so it's not the end of the world. Even after doing sales myself for 30 years I still don't like it, but I can be deal with it and internalized it in a healthy way.

I teach what I call the L.E.S.S. Method to Making More.

- Listen – when hearing a no or an objection you should start with letting them know you hear them. This can be nodding your head, making eye contact, or even saying words like "Okay."
- Empathize – Would be to say something like, "That makes sense", "Other people say that to me too" or "I understand." When a small child says these things it's both funny and impressive.

- <u>Solve</u> - Give them a solution to their objection. There really are no new objections, so role play out the objections and teach your kids to be prepared for them. Preparation in these areas will take you kids from reluctant selling to confident, conversational selling. They are going to hear, "I don't have the money," and at this point they might say, "They only cost this much and if you buy this many you get (fill in the blank)". They are going to hear other objections about time, not needing them, and having to ask someone else. All these things can have prepared solutions that your kid can share after listening and empathizing with the prospect. I do not suggesting your kids enter a hard sales process or nag people, but trying twice to sell is a good way to go for a kid. They pitch, they hear no, they L.E.S.S., then if they hear no again they move on. Have your kids go for no twice. A kid can up their sales by 20%-60% just by going for that second no.

- <u>Sell</u> – After you provided a solution to their objection ask for the sale again with what is called a tie down. You tell them how it is with a one word question at the end. This is a powerful language pattern to teach business people. An example is, "Cool, huh?", "Makes sense, doesn't it?", "You've got to like that, right?", "That helps, right?" After that final tie down, which is an invitation to buy, then the kid can just smilingly wait for the response, not saying anything else.

This is another great opportunity to role play with your kid. You be the prospect and say the objections you know your kid might hear. Give them the script or the words to use when overcoming that objection. Prepare you kid for no and what it really means. Set their expectation about selling. I always tell my kids that they are going to hear a lot of no's. I tell them they might hear 10 or 20 no's before they get that yes. That way, they aren't surprised or heart broken when they hear no. This is very important.

You really want your child to have some success the first time selling. This can really effect the future of your kid's attitude toward asking and selling things. The reality is that life is full of sales and persuasion. The sooner your child understands this the better off they will be. There is more on this topic throughout our business plans in the back of the book, on our website, and through our membership program. After all, this could be a whole book on its own and it is for grown entrepreneurs everywhere.

If marketing and advertising come first and selling comes second, then fulfillment (or customer service) comes third. Good customer service is another lost art that takes hard work and good training. I often say that there is always room in the market place for a new organization that combines good products and services with excellent customer care.

The power of smiling, making eye contact, under promising and over delivering are all good concepts to teach to your children. Point out good and bad customer service when you are at stores, restaurants, hotels, and airports. Teach your kids why you tip and when you tip. These are more great ongoing conversations to have about business and life. Guerrilla Parents teach not only about how to be a good entrepreneur but also how to be a good customer.

Fulfillment of goods and services is just as important as marketing and selling. Talk to your child about what companies do this well. I like the examples of Disney, Apple, Starbucks, or even FedEx. These companies sell an experience, or work in what I call "the experience economy". They want their clients and customers to have a magical or priceless experience.

I'll never forget when my daughter Nyah first came to Australia on business with me. She was surprised to see that the taxis didn't always help with the bags, the waiters didn't visit very often or refill our glasses, and people just weren't as hospitable. Don't get me wrong, I love my Australian friends, but their culture is different with higher wages and less tips. This has created a culture of less focus on customer service. We had some great conversations, my daughter and me.

These are all good conversations to have with your kids too. These concepts will change the way they see the world for the better.

You want things to start to click, for your kids to see the angles and ways businesses generate income. I'm sure some of your kids already do see opportunities and you already have discussions. Keep those conversations going. Guerrilla Parents have an attitude and lifestyle of exploring opportunities and money-making ideas.

Next we need to make your kids quitters…and finishers, but especially quitters. Sounds strange I know, but society messes up our kids more than you will ever know when it comes to quitting – and you are probably adding to that problem.

We should always strive to finish. Happiness is finishing. If you want more happiness just finish more of what you start. That's knowledge, but here is some more true information. Quitting is the Secret art of Winning.

The fact is that we have had the "quitters never win" mentality drilled into us for so long through so many books, speeches, and stories that we may forget that it's actually okay to quit.

Maybe you already have this knowledge about quitting. Of course, real wisdom is when people know when to apply best practices appropriately.

Here are a few people that know how to quit well:

1. Oprah quit Radio and went on to TV.
2. Michael Jordan quit baseball and went back to basketball.
3. Ronald Reagan quit acting and went into Politics.
4. Ellen DeGeneres quit acting and Stand-up comedy to become a Talk Show Host.

We can't quit everything all the time. Happiness is finishing, but it's also finishing the right things. The path to finishing the right things many times starts with quitting the wrong things.

Quitting may sound easy too, but it's not. Try quitting a bad habit, a bad relationship, or even a mediocre business. It's easier said than done…and you know it, don't you?

The best way to quit a project, a job, a sport, or even a business is to give it a set amount of time and evaluate everything only at that set time. Quitting is most dangerous when it's done in the heat of the moment. Quitting after a bad day, bad week, or even a bad month is rarely right.

Give it a season, three months, six months, or even a year before deciding whether or not you will quit. Make sure that you or your child are not running from something (like hard work) and that you are running towards something – a better, more proven opportunity.

Define success in everything that you and your child do. Know what it looks like. Understand what the metrics are in the area of life and business for your child that you may want to change someday. Then, and only then, monitor those metrics with predetermined timetables where you will reevaluate everything.

If your child starts to learn an instrument or play a sport, make sure they complete the agreed upon time or the season as a whole but always be willing to let your kids quit. Over all they must keep trying, always doing something to learn and grow, but allow them to quit under the right circumstances. Encourage quitting in the right way.

Don't ever just keep going for the sake of a "never say die" attitude. Some people have this romantic notion of going down with the ship, but that is rarely the right thing. Finishing is happiness. Finishing the right things is long term, sustainable happiness and that comes from learning the art of quitting!

Help your kids have these conversations and understand commitment to something, trying new things, and seeing something through in manageable time periods.

This book also has a dozen or so business plans to try out or discuss. They should create more great conversations, give your kids something to start, and maybe something to quit the right way. Really, they are just fun and easy ways to make money on a Saturday.

Guerrilla Parents experiment with businesses, have lots of conversations about opportunities, and challenge their child to dream without limits in an intellectual way when possible.

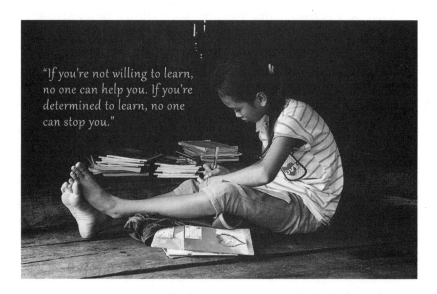

"If you're not willing to learn, no one can help you. If you're determined to learn, no one can stop you."

Chapter 12
Guerrilla Parenting Test

As a parent you have some tough decisions to make. You may think these tough decisions are about how you discipline, how to reward, and how to get your kids married off or into a good college. But those are not the decisions I am referring to.

There is actually one decision that is more important than anything else. Do you care more about helping your kids feel good, living the easiest life possible or do you care more about them becoming self-reliant adults, making good decisions and pursuing extraordinary lives?

Almost everything you do will lead to you fostering independence, work ethic, morality, and peace of mind or it will lead to dependence, a focus on immediate happiness, and the path of least resistance. The latter has become the status quo for most families and the former has become pretty unconventional, or in some cases considered mean.

There is the Average Parent and the Guerrilla Parent.

Some people have actually called me the meanest dad in the world, and many others say that my parenting style is downright cruel. Here are just a few of my beliefs that I get criticized over.

1. I never just let my kids win when competing against me.
2. I let my kids fail, and I rarely rescue them from life's circumstances.
3. I make them earn money for most things they want to do.

4. I refuse to save for their college education.
5. My family comes before everything including, sports, music, friends, school, and even church.

I'm not heartless, I promise. (Actually I'm confident that many of you reading agree with these point.) In fact, I express a lot of love to my children in a lot of ways. This Guerrilla Parenting style doesn't work without a lot of love in action, words, and deeds.

Your kids have to see you work for them, care for them, and love them unconditionally for them to know your intentions are true.

This is where parents get a little confused. They don't always understand the difference between working alongside them versus doing it for them. They don't always understand that not giving our children everything shows even more love.

By now you have a pretty good idea about what a Guerrilla Parent is, what they do, what they believe, and how they live and lead their children. There is a big difference between an Average Parent and a Guerrilla Parent.

Here are some examples of differences:

AP gives their kids things just because.
GP gives their kids some things but makes them work for most things.

AP wants their kid to have an easy life.
GP wants their kid to be strong enough to overcome.

AP wants their kid to be liked by others.
GP wants their kid to be okay with not being popular.

AP wants their kids to end up with lots of money.
GP wants their kid to earn a great life.

AP doesn't want their child to struggle.
GP wants them to be strong enough for the struggle.

AP wants their child to feel good.
GP wants their child to do what's right.

AP wants their child to get what the world owes them.
GP wants their child to work for their wants and needs.

AP wants their child to have parties and presents like everyone else.
GP wants their child to appreciate what matters most.

AP wants their child to answer to no one and for no one to get in their way.
GP wants their child to respect those that deserve respect.

AP responds to whining.
GP responds to work and winning.

AP wants to compensate for life's shortcomings.
GP wants to teach and prepare for life's shortcomings.

AP wants their child to win at all costs.
GP wants their child to know the cost of winning.

So are you an Average Parent or a Guerrilla Parent? Be honest with yourself. How did your parents do?

Let's expand on this with a test. How many of these questions can you answer TRUE?

True or False (For parents with a child over the age of 9)

1. My kid(s) exercise independence. T/F
2. My kid(s) earn their own money. T/F
3. My kid(s) have regular chores that they don't make any money doing. T/F
4. My kid(s) hear me say no often. T/F
5. My kid(s) don't expect me to pay for college and know they need to do their part for higher education. T/F
6. My kid(s) have sold products or services outside of the home. T/F
7. I spend time helping my kid(s) develop their talents. T/F
8. I spend considerable amounts of time communicating with my kid(s). T/F
9. My kid(s) have confidence and a healthy amount of self-esteem. T/F
10. My kid(s) fear very little and can take risks. T/F
11. I share my financial situation with my kids. T/F
12. My kids know how much it takes to run our home each month. T/F
13. I have marketing and advertising discussions with my kids. T/F
14. I role play sales situations with my kids. T/F
15. I make an effort to have entrepreneurial conversations with my kids. T/F
16. I recognize ambition in my kids and reward it. T/F
17. I help my kids try things for predetermined lengths of time and I'm not afraid to help them quit when the time is right. T/F
18. My kids have an idea of the kind of lifestyle they want when they grow up and what it will cost to have it. T/F

19. My kids point out and recognize ads that they like for the right reasons. T/F
20. My kids point out and recognize what good customer service is. T/F

If you can get 16 or more questions answered with TRUE then you are doing well as a Guerrilla Parent.

Chapter 13
Healthy Habits

I almost didn't include this chapter. You must be overwhelmed with diet and exercise information. I know I am. The simple truth is that it is a huge factor in your child's moment to moment success. This whole book is about lifestyles and attitudes that will put all the odds in your favor of raising a successful kid. The book would be incomplete without discussing diet, exercise, and sleep.

The truth is that so many of our children's problems these days are amplified by poor eating habits. For many kids, bad nutrition results in a child with a short fuse that can't focus or even sit still! As a society, we are responding with new diagnoses of ADD and ADHD that are typically treated with medications that have many side effects.

I know this is a sensitive subject, and I don't claim to be a doctor of any kind. I know that some kids, and even adults for that matter, truly need medication, but this seems to be the growing quick fix that leaves many other things left broken.

Health expert, Erleen Tilton, and author of the upcoming book, *The 7 Secrets of Healthy Happy People (available Spring 2015)*, experienced many health challenges first hand in her life. Her struggle to regain her well-being by eliminating what was killing her has been such an inspiration to many.

In 1980, as a young mother Erleen found herself in a serious state of depression accompanied with frequent migraines, allergies, over a dozen breast lumps, hypoglycemia, anemia, and more. Under the close supervision of a naturopathic physician who recommended a strict regimen of healthier foods, cleansing, concentrated whole food supplements, and nature's medicines (which she followed faithfully), in six months Erleen's health was completely reversed to being full of energy and free from any problems.

Most of us have bought into the 'junk food and medicines' lifestyle. With that comes the oppression, which she clearly experienced, of feeling trapped emotionally and physically in our dysfunctional bodies without answers. Not only did she overcome and maintain a healthy body by adhering to healthy lifestyle principles ever since, but she has also come to understand that the simple truths that could set us free are found in nature...made by the creator of our bodies...and may not be plainly evident unless searched for.

"When I saw the transformation in my own health simply by understanding and applying the principles of a wellness lifestyle, I realized that this is such a key for our struggling, sick world who know not where to find the answers. In nature, we find these simple success secrets."

Recently the National Mental Health Association stated, "The truth is that preschool aged children are the fastest growing age group being prescribed anti-depressants." Think about that...if our preschool age children are on antidepressants, what will their lives look like during their teen years, or, worse yet, as adults?

One of my daughters was diagnosed with ADD around 11 years of age. As she became a teen, there were several conversations in and around my family about whether or not she should take some kind of medication. I had concerns about some of the side effects, like the potential to stunt growth. I was also concerned about labels and beliefs that a child can develop by accepting a title that could also work as a crutch in life.

For our family, we wanted to try everything else first. We wanted to invest more time as parents, help her recognize her strengths and weaknesses, and ultimately make sure she was healthy in every other way. This took a lot of work on our part and hers, but we avoided those labels and medication, teaching our daughter that she can do hard things. This may be one of the most important lesson a person can ever learn.

I am not saying that every parent, child, or family will be able to avoid all medication, but shouldn't we at least try? Consider these statistics:

- 65% of all American adults are overweight. More than 31% of adults in the U.S. are obese and are at risk for chronic disease. (news-medical.net)
- The percentage of obese kids aged 6 to 11 in the United States increased from 7% in 1980 to almost 18% in 2012. (cdc.gov)
- Developmental disabilities are on the rise in the U.S. Between 1997 and 2008, the number of school –aged children diagnosed with autism, ADHD, or other developmental disability rose by 17%. (cbsnews.org) Some studies also indicate that poor nutrition early in life may lead to learning disabilities later in life. (kidshealth.org)

Childhood is an important time to learn about all the habits that will make them self-reliant, happy adults. These habits include not only the ones we've discussed in earlier chapters, but also how to properly care for our bodies so we can be healthy mentally and physically.

For our bodies to function properly, there must be an adequate supply of nutrients: vitamins, minerals, fiber, enzymes, and more. There are lots of ways to get these into your body, but a first big step is just to include more raw vegetables and fruits in your diet. Although I don't do this all the time, I also try to omit a lot of high sugar and high carbohydrate foods that are processed. This not only should be an important focus for any parent who wants to raise healthy children, but should especially be considered before turning to medications as a solution for health problems.

Like I spoke of earlier in this book, we need to have conversations and participate in certain activities to raise self-reliant children, but this is really hard to do if they can't concentrate or comprehend. A child must be able to listen, to focus, and become self-aware. Children, as well as adults, can never change without first becoming self-aware.

Without becoming self-aware, we won't be able to recognize our tendencies, bad habits, and warning signs of terrible things to come so that we might improve ourselves. Children and teenagers can best do this if they have the longer fuse that comes from a healthy life. Kids that constantly melt down should first try better diet, exercise, and getting the right amount of quality sleep.

To become a productive adult, we need to be able to work under pressure, make important decision in stressful situations, and have the energy to focus for long periods of time. This is much easier to do when our kids first form these habits before becoming adults.

One of the reasons that this issue is so convoluted is that we don't always physically see the signs of pour nutrition. Many kids look thin or proportionate, which is how most people judge health, unfortunately. A better way would be to look for warning signs of constant crying, complaining, meltdowns, and other extreme moods that seem uncontrollable.

If you are like me, you are frustrated with all the constantly changing reports and information on what is really good for you. I am more of a moderation guy, which is admittedly risky. After all, I don't expect my kids not to ever have desserts or treats. Some people say I'm too extreme because of what foods I restrict in our family diet. Others say I am risking my kids' lives because I'm not careful enough about what they eat.

My father became a vegan years ago, but that is too extreme for me. My mother-in-law has celiac disease, so she avoids gluten. As in these examples and more, sometimes going without certain foods is because of taste and preference while other times it's a vital need for health and wellness. Some kids may have a problem with gluten and others may have a problem with dairy. If it's not an extreme problem there may be room for variables, however, if there is an extreme problem, food choices could make a huge difference between agitated and cool-tempered, depressed or energetic, learning issues and a focused child, behavioral issues and an obedient child.

Just like everything else in this book, you have to parent every kid a little different. It's hard when every child can respond a little differently to diets, discipline, and motivating factors. Regardless, in this area as with all others, you need to customize your parenting as much as possible.

Here are some facts about my family's eating style and habits.

- We eat meat, but not all the time. I would say 1/3 of our meals have some kind of meat in it.
- We rarely drink soda, maybe once a month. This is a huge problem for most families in my opinion.
- We drink caffeine even less, maybe once a quarter. Some of my kids have never had caffeine.
- We never drink coffee, espresso, or any other kind of hot, caffeinated drinks.
- We never drink alcohol of any kind.
- We rarely eat out.
- We rarely use medicines or go to the doctor. Instead, we opt for essential oils and various tinctures that are made from plant life.
- Some of us drink no milk at all, but we buy both 1% and whole milk for those that do.

- It's not uncommon for us to have brown rice and whole wheat bread.
- We do some calorie counting and look out for different types of fats, sugars, colorings, and additives.
- We let the kids have snacks, but try to have them snack on fruit between meals. We are not afraid to let a child go without if they refuse to eat what's for dinner.
- I like almonds, fruit, and health bars for snacks. I try to set an example.
- I encourage my kids to hide sugary stuff from me, which is fun to them.
- Salads, beans, and other vegetables are common in my home.

Exercise is important too. Dr. Michael Omidi, co-founder of The Children's Obesity Fund said, "It is becoming increasingly obvious that the lack of physical exercise in children is the main culprit in the startling rise of childhood obesity, heart disease, diabetes, and all other types of preventable medical conditions."

It's not uncommon for my kids to have to do certain athletic or physical activities before being able to spend time inside or with technology. They can choose between various activities that included running, biking, swimming, jumping on the trampoline, and other combinations of pushups, sit ups, and jumping jacks.

To get the blood pumping, more oxygen deep into the lungs, and a little sweat forming are great things for kids. It makes them have more of an appetite, better sleep, and stay out of trouble. It also helps them discover other talents and earn the respect of peers as they excel in sports. All of these things increase a child's confidence as well.

Eating and exercising will both make your kids sleep better. As a parent you must recognize when your child is grouchy and quick to break down. Some kids need to sleep more than others, especially at different times in their life. Regardless of the age, sleep is important. Having night time Expression Rituals are important.

Brushing teeth, going to the restroom, reading stories, tucking in, and maybe even singing songs can all be helpful in preparing a child to sleep. My wife is great at this, but appointments and business travel many times make it hard for me to do this as consistently as I would like.

I also find that giving kids alarms and letting them choose the exact time they wake up (within a preapproved range) can also be very helpful and foster independence in your child. Ultimately, it seems more like their choice to sleep and wakeup which is always good.

I could easily make this a whole book in and of itself, and many already have. Nevertheless, the most important thing to know here is that having a well-balanced, focused, and highly adaptable kid is more easily possible if they are healthy in every way possible. We are constantly learning about the important role food and drinks play in our lives. Guerrilla Parents are always learning and studying life's healthiest choices.

Remember, like everything else I teach in this book, healthy lifestyles are a habit worth forming. Look at what's in your fridge and cupboards right now. Is it what you would want someone else to see or would you be embarrassed by the contents? What did you and your family eat this last week? If you had to write it out like a menu, would you be ashamed to show it to someone? Plan your meals and exercise like you do your entrepreneurial activities with your kids. Guerrilla Parents practice healthy habits and lifestyles in all aspects of life.

Chapter 14
The Pursuit of Parenting

I'm not sure we ever truly capture the science of perfect parenting. It's more of an art that never ends. It's similar to how doctors and attorney have a practice. The learning never stops. Just because you know something doesn't mean you always do it either. Writing this book reminded me of a ton of things that I want to do better in my own family.

You can't be too hard on yourself, but I do encourage some goals. Set some time aside to have conversations. Take time to teach with the visual aids the book provides you. Chart your child's successes and failures so that you both might learn. What good Guerrilla Parenting really comes down to is parents spending quality time with their kids doing entrepreneurial activities and having entrepreneurial conversations.

Remember to take care of yourself, too. The oxygen mask goes on you first, then your child. You may have noticed that the better you understand entrepreneurial topics yourself the better you may do at this Guerrilla Parenting. This means you need to understand what it means to be an entrepreneur. I also suggest you read these books for a better understanding of what it means to be self-employed, an independent contractor, a small business owner, and ultimately an entrepreneur.

1. The original *Guerrilla Marketing* book by Jay Conrad Levinson
2. *Guerrilla Rainmakers* by Jay Conrad Levinson and David T. Fagan
3. *The E-Myth* and/or *The E-Myth Revisited*
4. Just about any book written by Dan Kennedy. No joke.
5. *Conquer the Chaos* by Clate Mask and Scott Martineau
6. *The Entrepreneur Mind* by Kevin Johnson
7. *The $100 Startup* by Chris Guillebeau

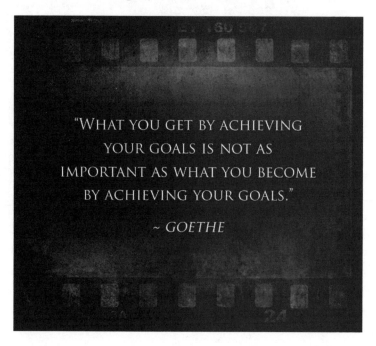

"WHAT YOU GET BY ACHIEVING
YOUR GOALS IS NOT AS
IMPORTANT AS WHAT YOU BECOME
BY ACHIEVING YOUR GOALS."

~ *GOETHE*

Granted, you don't have to be an entrepreneur to raise an entrepreneur, but remember it's an attitude at home, a customized education through the home, and an ongoing lifestyle beyond the home that makes it all possible. You must customize your education before you can customize your child's education.

And your kid does not have to be an entrepreneur to reach the higher goal of this book, which is for everyone to become more self-reliant as we raise more generations of creative problem solvers and action takers. There are plenty of great jobs where people can get paid to do what they love.

We have created other programs through our website and through Facebook so that we can continue to share what we learn. There are also teleseminars and webinars where you can get info, coaching, and advice in the realm of Guerrilla Parenting.

Reach out to us. We love to hear from our readers. We take a lot of hits for our GP beliefs, so hearing from like-minded parents is very fulfilling.

You can reach us by email at david@davidtfagan.com, Facebook by searching 'Guerrilla Parenting'.

We want to hear about your kids' success stories. We even have a very sophisticated, upscale Teen Entrepreneur Summer Camp that your child may want to attend someday. We prefer they earn the money to go themselves and even show them how.

After all, we practice what we preach…Guerrilla Parenting.

Bonus Business Plans for Kids and Teens

As a parent, you're a chauffeur, a chef, a housekeeper, and a psychologist. As a Guerrilla Parent, you're also your child's agent, their teacher, and their mentor. You may have to help with the booking process, promoting your kids to safe venues, and helping them learn the basics.

We have often been asked, "Which is the best business?" This is hard because it again depends on how much you want to be involved and the attitude, interests, and abilities of your child.

Some kids love detailed work, so the virtual assistant or enchilada business plans might be best for them. The candy shop or DJ businesses may work best for kids that are socially outgoing. Some kids love being outside, so the dog grooming or car wash businesses might work best for them. The jewelry making or music lesson business plans may work best for children that are creative.

The area you live in will also greatly affect what businesses do well. Our kids have had a lot of success doing the VA business, but in our area they get paid $12 an hour to watch kids. When they babysit, they don't have any long lasting obligations like they do with the VA service, so they'll often choose to babysit instead.

Whatever you and your child decide to try, remember to give it a pre-determined amount of time and then re-evaluate. Each of these plans will help them learn a lot about themselves and their skills, interests, and talents. And remember to have fun!

Business Plan for a Door-to-Door Car Wash

General Description

This business is perfect for kids aged 8 – 17 years old.

Mission Statement: To provide a necessary service to people too busy or unable to perform this task themselves.

Goals and Objectives: The goal is to create a business that provides a good source of income by working weekends and summers. The objective is to build a reputation for great service and increase sales each month via word of mouth.

Marketing: This service will be marketed to neighbors, housewives and mothers, friends' parents, and anyone with a dirty car, truck, or motorcycle!

Competitive strengths are in convenience to the customer and performing all the little details important to each customer.

Pricing structure is donations or a fair price.

What this business teaches – Face to face communication, how to work fast to earn more money quickly, how to face rejection and go on to the next job, making a sales presentation.

How we've used this plan – This business plan is one of the first ones we used and is a proven money maker. Jordan earned hundreds of dollars to go to New York City with this business.

Operational Plan

Inventory: What's Needed

- Large mop bucket on wheels
- 6-10 towels
- Hose sprayer attachment
- Squeegee
- Car wash sponges

- Liquid dish detergent
- Tire cleaner
- Window cleaner
- Hose (just in case)
- Stepladder
- Cash box or money bag

What to Do

This is a good business to do on a warm day because people don't want to leave their houses to get their cars washed when it's hot. Saturdays are when more people are typically home.

Have your child get all of the supplies together, and put them in the bucket. Load it all up in the car, and help your child find a street with a lot of mature trees and cars parked in the driveway or on the street. Big trees usually mean the cars will have more leaves and bird droppings on them.

Start at the beginning of the street and go to each house. Your job will be to stay in eye-sight of the customer, but you should let your child go to the door themselves. They're going to get a lot of no's and no answers. That's okay because they'll get some yes's too. It's their job to find the yes's.

They should knock on the door and give the script. If they are excited and show enthusiasm, people will know that this is something they want to do.

When they get a yes, they should signal to you and hook up the spray nozzle to the person's hose or to theirs if they don't have one. Your child should make sure the bucket is filled up about half way and has enough soap bubbles.

The next step is to get the car wet and start washing with the sponge. They should try to get the top of the car or have you help them. If they are using a stepladder, they need to be careful that it doesn't get wet to prevent slipping and falling. You should hold the ladder if they do use one, for safety's sake. Your child needs to make sure that they get it clean, but this shouldn't take more than 7-10 minutes, if that.

Next they'll use the squeegee and soap to do a quick wash on the windows and tires, but your child shouldn't take too long because they'll have to wash them again. They can then spray the car off with the hose, making sure to get all the soap off.

Drying the car off with the towels is the next step, but they should leave the windows and tires wet. Using the window cleaner and squeegee to give the windows a good shine, they should try not to get the cleaner on the car. If they do, they need to wipe it off. A quick spray of the tires with the tire cleaner and they can use the sponge to get it clean. Pick one older towel that they will use all day to wipe the tires dry. Plan on this getting ruined.

Return the hose to the proper place, and wind it up. Thank the customer for allowing you to wash their car and collect the money.

Secure the money in the cash box or money bag.

Go to the next house, and try it again!

How to Make it Safe

As a parent, you don't need to go to the door with your child--and actually it is better if you don't so that your child can give the pitch by themselves – but you should be close enough that the person at the door can see you. This will help them feel more comfortable that your child isn't alone and assure them that they are going to get a good car wash.

Make sure your child knows the dangers of the chemicals they are using, and make sure they don't get it in their eyes or mouth.

Script

Hi my name is (child's name here), and I'm doing a young entrepreneur project. I'm earning money for (whatever sport, project, or item they want to purchase). Would you allow me to wash your car?

If they ask how much it is say, "I'm taking donations, so it's however much you think the job I do is worth."

Marketing Plan

The main methods of marketing will be word of mouth and referrals. Be sure they take their own business cards with them and hand one out to each customer.

Your child may also want to create a simple flyer that they can post in your neighborhood with a list of the services they provide, the days they are available to work, and your home phone number. Be careful of where they place it, and consider at what age you would allow your child to put their own cell phone number on the flyer. It should mention that they will be hand washing each car, refer to their attention to detail, and that the cleaning products they use are safe for a vehicle's finish – this differentiates their business from the competition. Use of color to grab people's attention in the flyer is a great idea; they can print on colored paper or use full color images.

Their next job will be to spread the word of their business to school mates, local businesses, your church congregation, relatives, neighbors, and friends. They will need to keep their business cards and flyers handy to give out.

Don't forget they can market online, too. Posting to their Facebook, Twitter, and Instagram accounts that they are now the proud owner of their own business is a good start.

Finances

It's a good idea to keep a cash box or money bag in your car in which to put their car wash proceeds. Your child should also start out with different denominations of money so they can make change.

At the end of the day, help them count up their earnings and expenses. Some things they'll want to keep track of in a spreadsheet or manual table are:

- Cost of supplies
- Loan amount for startup costs (if applicable)
- How much money they collected
- The number of houses they went to
- How many no answers, no's, and yes's they got
- How much product they used and how much is left
- How much time they spent getting supplies
- How much time they spent working

Tracking these numbers will allow you to figure out:

- Profit
- Close rate
- Cost per wash
- Hourly rate of pay
- Many other figures as well

If you provided the money for their supplies, have them pay you back from the proceeds of their first day or split it up over a few days of work. You may also want to charge for the gas it takes you to drive the neighborhood if you want them to bear the full cost.

Make sure to help them split their money into the money envelope or bag system appropriately. Cost of supplies for future car washes should be set aside as short term savings. If they're old enough, they can open a savings account at the bank and make regular deposits in order to earn interest.

Business Plan for a Chicken Enchilada Sale

General Description

This business is perfect for kids aged 8 – 17 years old, especially if they like to cook

Mission Statement: To provide a tasty and affordable lunch to busy office employees and other workers.

Goals and Objectives: The goal is to create a business that provides a good source of income during the summer months. The objective is to build a reputation for great food and encourage repeat business.

Marketing: Chicken enchilada lunches will be marketed to people who work in office complexes or buildings or family and church friends.

Competitive strengths are in convenience to the customer and providing a home-cooked meal to replace fast food lunches.

Pricing structure is based on cost of supplies; $15 per dozen is suggested at today's prices.

What this business teaches – Sanitation, not buying too much product, estimating costs and profits, face to face and phone communication, making a sales presentations, and making a presentation for a loan.

How we've used this plan – This business plan is one that Jill and her sisters used as teenagers and one that is a favorite in our house. It's been used to pay for girl's camp money, car accidents, trips to Australia and Flagstaff, and of course spending money for clothes and fun.

Operational Plan

Inventory: What's Needed

Ingredients per 3 dozen Chicken Enchiladas:

- 3-14 oz cans cream of chicken soup
- 16 oz sour cream
- 2 cups grated cheese (Cheddar, Colby jack, or longhorn)
- 3 chicken breasts, cooked and shredded
- ½ to 1 onion, minced
- 1-4 oz can green chilies
- 36 corn tortillas
- Oil

Other Supplies:

- Gloves
- Clean plastic tablecloth (optional)
- Aluminum Foil
- 10 lb block ice
- Address labels (3111 or 3113 Avery)
- Phone (to get orders)
- Ice Chest
- Car (to get ingredients and to get and deliver orders)
- Enchilada Order Form
- Office Order Form
- The Script

What to Do

Set aside two days for this job. For the first time, don't take too many orders, or it will turn into an overwhelming job. A good number is 9 or 12 dozen.

First Day

Your child should start by figuring out where they are going to get their orders from. Once they print up the order form and hit the phones, they can call people from church, their friends' parents, family friends, some of your work friends, etc. Make sure that they are professional and that they let the customers know that this is a business. They should pick a specific goal or trip they're working toward so that the customers will be more likely to buy, like a plane ticket to a fun location, a ticket to an entrepreneurial event, going to camp, buying clothes, saving for college, or donations to a charity or needy family. Before they start with a live person, they need to practice the script a few times to get familiar with it.

If they are thinking about selling in office buildings, they'll need to attach an Office Order Form to a large manila envelope for each building. They'll write down who ordered, how many dozen they ordered, how much they need to pay, and if they're interested in ordering next time. They need to have one person be responsible for collecting for the office so that when they drop off the enchiladas, they can count the money and leave.

They should try to get orders by the threes so that they don't have leftover materials that eat into their profits. Once they have their orders, they need to go and buy their materials. Make sure that they have a sanitized area to work from. This is a great opportunity to help them learn all the steps they need to take to keep their work area clean and safe. They also may consider covering the table with a clean plastic disposable tablecloth to make clean-up fast and easy. When handling food, they should wear disposable gloves and keep long hair braided and all hair out of their face. They'll be tempted, but remind them not to lick anything. You will also want to make sure that when they're not using the ingredients, they are kept refrigerated. Teach them to wash their hands and utensils often.

Once prep is done, they need to cook the chicken, keeping it separated by batch so that they will have the right amount. First they'll boil the chicken until its tender. This should take about 30 minutes per batch, but they can cook several batches at once. They will put the heat on high until it starts to boil and then turn down gradually to a medium low temperature. It should stay simmering the whole time. After it is cooked, they'll need to take it out of the water and let it cool until it is warm. They will then shred the chicken and store it in a sealed container in the fridge until the next day.

Second Day

They start the day by preparing their clean work area, putting their hair back, and putting their gloves on clean hands. In a large bowl, they get to mix all ingredients for one batch except for the tortillas. Once mixed, they can separate the mixture into three equal sized bowls. In each bowl, they will draw two lines to separate it into quarters. Each quarter should make three enchiladas.

Next they will line a 9 x 13 pan with heavy duty aluminum foil, leaving 4-6 inches on each side to close it up. Preparing the 12 tortillas by brushing them lightly with oil is next, and then they should be placed in the microwave for 1 minute on each side. They'll put 1/3 of the chicken mixture into the middle of the tortilla, roll, and place them into the pan.

After 12 tortillas are rolled, it's time for them to fold the sides of the foil up to the top of the pile the long way. Then they'll want to fold the short ends up to the center in a neat package. Next, they get to put the package into the ice chest or the fridge.

This is when they can wash off the utensils and bowls and make another batch and repeat until all enchiladas are rolled.

If they'd like, they can make up address labels with their contact information and attach them to the foil so that people can let them know if they're interested in re-ordering.

Delivery

Put the enchiladas they are delivering into the ice chest. They'll want to staple their order form to a manila envelope and bring some change if possible. Obviously you'll want to be part of the delivery process, driving and escorting them into each office and back to the car if their age dictates this.

When you get to the house or the office, be sure to have your child count the money and thank them for their order. They should let them know that they will be doing this again in a few weeks and gauge their interest in re-ordering. Check off the order as paid and your budding entrepreneur can mark down if the customers want to order in the future.

How to Make it Safe

Reinforce good hygiene practices before and during the cooking experience.

Watch your children while they are cooking on the stove.

Make sure food is refrigerated and stored properly.

Only sell to people you know or go door to door and into office buildings with your child.

Phone Script

Hi my name is (your child's name) from (however you know them). Is this a good time to talk? I'm doing a young entrepreneur project and I'm earning money for (their project name). I'm selling chicken and cheese enchiladas. These are not just plain cheese, like some schools sell. This is a time tested recipe that has been used for more than 30 years and they're really good. They are $15 per dozen and you can order them with or without onions. Which would you prefer? (Wait for them to answer) And how many dozen do you want? (Wait for them to answer) Thank you so much! These will be ready tomorrow after (time you're available). What time do you want to pick them up or would you prefer delivery?

Office Script

Hi, my name is _(your child's name)_ and I'm doing a young entrepreneur project. I'm earning money for _(project or trip name)_. I'm wondering if I can talk to the people in your office. (Wait for people to gather or go individually to each.)

Hi, my name is _(your child's name)_ and I'm doing a young entrepreneur project. I'm earning money for _(project or trip name)_. I'm selling chicken and cheese enchiladas. These are not just plain cheese, like some schools sell. This is a time tested recipe that has been used for more than 30 years and they're really good. I'll deliver tomorrow by _____. They are $15 per dozen and you can order them with or without onions. I'll pass this form around. Please write down which would you prefer and how many dozen you want? (Have them write down the information.)

Is there someone that would be willing to hold the money for everyone in the office until I deliver them tomorrow? (Hand that person the envelope with the Office Order Form attached and ask them to paper clip cash for each order together.)

Thank you all so much! I'll see you tomorrow after _____.

Marketing Plan

The main method of marketing will be their own sales skills and referrals from previous customers. Be sure they take their business cards with them to hand out to each customer when you deliver their order.

They need to spread the word of their business to school mates, local businesses, your church congregation, relatives, neighbors, and friends. Teach them to keep their business cards and flyers handy to give out. Everyone needs to eat, so their target market is nearly unlimited.

Help them be proactive and find new business opportunities. If your neighborhood is having a block party or a friend's parents are planning a get-together with other adults, suggest they offer their chicken enchiladas for sale. Are your neighbors going to have a big yard sale? They might want to bake several batches and offer them to hungry shoppers.

Finances

The manila envelopes as suggested provide a good way to keep their day's earnings in one place.

Keep track of them in a spreadsheet or a manual table so you and they know how much they can earn, and how much they have made.

At the end of the day, help them count up their earnings by location. This helps your child determine which places are best to return to in the future and gives them a better idea of what customers to target. Some other things they'll want to keep track of in a spreadsheet or manual table are:

- Cost of supplies
- Loan amount for startup costs (if applicable)
- How much money they collected
- The number of business complexes they went to
- How many no's and yes's they got
- How much time they spent getting supplies
- How much time they spent preparing and delivering

Tracking these numbers will allow you to figure out:

- Profit
- Close rate
- Cost per dozen
- Hourly rate of pay
- And many other figures as well

If you provided the money for their supplies, have them pay you back from these proceeds. You may also want to charge for the gas it takes you to drive them to get and deliver orders if you want them to bear the full cost.

Make sure to help them split their money into the money envelope or bag system appropriately. Cost of supplies for future enchilada sales should be set aside as short term savings. They can also start watching for when supply items come on sale to reduce their upfront costs and increase their profit margin. If they're old enough, they can open a savings account at the bank and make regular deposits in order to earn interest.

Business Plan for a Craigslist Upsell

General Description

This business is perfect for kids aged 10 – 17 years old.

Mission Statement: To provide a necessary service to people too busy or unable to perform this task themselves.

Goals and Objectives: The goal is to create a business that provides a good source of income by working weekends and summers. The objective is to take items people don't want and sell them for a profit.

Marketing: This service will be marketed to people in your local area on Craigslist.

Competitive strengths are in selling items when the customer is ready to buy and delivery to those that can't pick things up.

Pricing structure is what the market will bear.

What this business teaches – Face to face communication, how to price objects to make money quickly, negotiating a price.

How we've used this plan – This business has been used by several of my kids, but mostly by my daughter to pay for her trip to Peru.

Operational Plan

Inventory: What's Needed

- Computer
- Internet connection
- Cleaning supplies
- Dolly

- Large vehicle/truck to pick items up
- Phone

What to Do

This business works best in a large city or suburban area because there will be more people looking to get rid of things quickly and more people looking to buy items at a particular time. (This may be slightly more difficult in smaller areas that don't have as many free items or people looking to buy.) This is also a great business to do on weekends and at the end of the month when people are trying to move out.

Help your child look for items on Craigslist that are listed for free in your area (there's a section under the 'for sale' area that says 'free'). They should look for things that they have room enough to store, something they can physically pick up by themselves or with help from an adult, and things that will sell quickly.

When they find something that is in really good shape and that they have the capacity to pick up (strength, room to store, vehicle that it can fit in), search the same item in the 'for sale' section of Craigslist. Look at the range of low, high, and middle prices for this item to determine what the selling range is.

While looking in the 'for sale' section, your child should note how their item is similar and different. This will help determine how much they will list it for. They should also look at how many similar items are listed and how long they have been listed. If there are numerous items that are very similar to theirs that have been listed for more than two weeks, it may not be a good time to sell the item they're considering. This doesn't mean that they shouldn't pick it up if it's a really great item. It just means that they may have to store it for a longer time in order to get the price they're looking for. This always has to be a consideration.

Other information to look at is the descriptions people use in the 'for sale' area. Your child should make sure to ask for similar information from the lister of the item so their ad will be more likely to entice buyers to respond to it.

Once your child has found that there is a market for the item they're wanting to sell, they should contact the lister of that item by whatever is the preferred method. Make sure that they do this as soon after the listing has gone up as possible so the item will most likely still be available. When contact with the lister is made, make sure your child is the one doing it. Remember that this is their business and they need to be seen as the contact and decision maker. You should be in the same room to help them with anything that they need. They will want to ask the following questions. There may be others as well, but this is a great start:

- Do the pictures in the ad reflect the current condition of the item?
- What are the dimensions of the item?
- When is the item available for pick up?
- What is the address for pick up and is it searchable on Google Maps?
- Is there anything I need to know about the item that wasn't listed in the ad?

If the lister lets them know the item is immediately available, your child should arrange for pick up within 30 to 60 minutes. Most people on Craigslist have found that pickups are unreliable, so make sure the item gets taken care of as soon as possible to ensure the item is still available.

Before leaving to get the item, have your child download the pictures of the listed item onto their computer. Often, there isn't an opportunity to take great pictures of the item when you get to the pickup location or once you get it to your house for storage. Having these pictures is a guarantee that you'll have something to put in your relisting ad.

You'll also want to help your child put in whatever equipment they'll need to get the item loaded. Some things they may want to use are furniture or piano dollies, moving blankets, or sliders that you can put under the feet of the furniture. All of these will make the job of moving big items easier and safer.

Once you get to the location for pick up, have your child do the talking. They can let the person know that they appreciate the opportunity to help them get rid of the item and that it will be put to good use. They may not necessarily want to say that they are going to immediately relist the item, but they can say they will use the item in their business. This is a good opportunity to hand the lister a card and tell them to call if they have any other unwanted items.

If the pictures on the ad weren't great, now is the time to get good images for your ad. Make sure your child takes pictures of the front, back, top, and sides as well as any dents or dings that may influence the price. Your child should also take measurements now to make sure it will fit in your vehicle. Write these down so you can put them in your ad. Have your child test out the item so that they know exactly what they're getting. They should also decide if it will need fixing or cleaning so they know what it will take to sell. Just because you went to look at the item doesn't mean you have to pick it up if you don't think it will sell or it isn't what you were looking for. Neither you nor your child will be happy with a garage full of stuff you can't sell!

Once you decide it's worth the effort, carefully help your child load the item onto the appropriate equipment and into the vehicle. Your child should thank the lister and remind them to contact them for additional items for consideration.

When you get home, help your child unload the item. Clean the item if needed and take any pictures you weren't able to at the original location. Then store the item in an area in which it will be safe until it is sold. Your child may want to cover it with a tarp if it's outside so it will be protected from the elements.

If you picked up the item on a weekday, this gives your child more of an opportunity to fix or clean it up before the weekend. If not, this will need to be a fast process so they can get it relisted as quickly as possible. The weekend is the most likely time an item will get purchased, so get it up fast.

Help your child create an account on Craigslist, which is free, so they can list their items for sale. Make sure that they don't list an exact address and that they use a cell or house number that will be safe for them to get calls on.

They should put a lot of detail into the description and add the best images. Whatever stood out to them when they were looking at 'for sale' items can be used here. If the item is in great shape and is better than most other similar items, list it on the high end of the price range. If it has some wear and tear, list it in the middle range of prices. They should also put in the description that they will deliver for a fee and gas money. This will allow more people the opportunity to buy their item.

When people respond to their ad, your child should be the one to do the talking. It will be helpful if they have role played this a bit in advance. Make sure to discuss negotiating the price. They will feel more comfortable if they know what their stated bottom line is, as well as their real bottom line. For example, a buyer might say, "You're asking $200 but I can only pay $150. Will you take that?" Even though $150 might be your child's real bottom line, they should say, "Let's split the difference at $175." The buyer may agree to this middle negotiation. If they still insist they can't go more than $150, your child has still met their bottom line.

Have your child set up a pick up time for when you or another adult will be available. They should ensure they have varying amounts of change so that there won't be any issues for payment. When the buyer gets there, you should be in attendance the whole time, but your child should do the talking. Have your child show the item and answer any questions. They should collect payment before the buyer loads the item onto their vehicle.

Your child should let them know that they run this as a business and what they're saving for if appropriate then give them a business card. They can let the buyer know they come across a lot of objects and ask if there's anything else the buyer is looking for. If there is something, your child should ask for their contact information and keep this in mind for future business.

How to Make it Safe

As a parent, you should let your child do all the talking, but you or another adult need to be physically present when your child is meeting with or talking to listers or buyers. You should also help your child with any heavy lifting, reminding them to lift in a safe manner.

Finances

It's a good idea to keep start out with different denominations of money so they can make change.

Help your child track their earnings and expenses. You may consider charging your child a labor cost if you are the one doing the heavy lifting. If you provided the money for their cleaning supplies, have them pay you back from the proceeds of their first sale. You may also want to charge for the gas it takes you to pick up or deliver items and a per diem fee for storage if you want them to bear the full cost.

Make sure to help them split their money into the money envelope or bag system appropriately. Cost of supplies or storage fees for future sales should be set aside as short term savings. If they're old enough, they can open a savings account at the bank and make regular deposits in order to earn interest.

Business Plan for a Virtual Assistant Service

General Description

This business is perfect for kids aged 12 – 17 years old.

Mission Statement: To provide a necessary service to people too busy or unable to perform this task themselves for a less expensive fee than traditional VA services.

Goals and Objectives: The goal is to create a business that provides a good source of income by working afternoons, weekends, and summers. The objective is to build a reputation for great service and increase sales each month via word of mouth and social networking.

Marketing: This service will be marketed mainly on social media but also to neighbors, friends' parents, parents' friends, and anyone with a small business!

Competitive strengths are in convenience to the customer and allowing them to speak to someone that understands their needs.

Pricing structure can be an hourly rate or a set fee per service. Typical hourly rates are between $8 and $11 an hour.

What this business teaches –Making a sales presentation, email and phone communication, customer service, reliability, and how to be creative.

If your child loves graphic design or technology, this is a great job for them. Keep in mind that this business involves an ongoing commitment to customers. It's not like some business plans where they do interact with a client once.

How we've used this plan – Our daughter, Jordan, had such success with this plan that she started her own company, Hire A Teen Today. She has earned thousands of dollars with this business plan.

Operational Plan

Inventory: What's Needed

- Laptop
- Image membership (optional)
- Internet connection
- Phone

What to Do

Find people who are in need of virtual assistant services through word of mouth, social media, and friends (see more in the marketing section). Once you find someone in need, offer to work on a project for free that has a high perceived value. By this, I mean it should appear to take a lot of time, to involve a skill set that may not come easy to someone, or be tedious in nature. By doing it for free you accomplish several things. First, you earn the right to ask for their business in the future. Second, you show them the quality of your work, your communication skills on a project, and being able to deliver on a deadline. Whatever you create for them you can also show to other people. Having a portfolio of your work is paramount.

In addition, even when you're working for free to prove yourself, ask for a video testimonial. Once you have enough written and video testimonials, along with your portfolio or work, the odds will be much more in your favor of being hired as a virtual assistant for pay.

To learn the various skills and job duties you'll be offering, shadow someone that is already doing them. Many people are willing to let you do this if you ask. High tech programing and graphic design can have way too much of a learning curve for most kids and teens, but there are many other job duties of a VA that can be picked up fairly easily. Whether you're looking for business or somebody to shadow, ask yourself these two questions: 'Who do I know?' or 'Who do I know who knows who I want to know?' Who do you know that has the profession you want to assist? Or who do you know that assists people in these professions? Or who do you know that knows people that do these two things.

How to Make it Safe

As a parent, you don't need to be on every phone call, but you should be in the same room so that you can assist with any questions your child may have. If your child is going to a physical location to shadow someone, make sure it's someone you know personally and consider staying there while they learn. Always know who your child is communicating with.

Marketing Plan

Look to target small business owners and professional agents who typically have a need for an assistant. This includes insurance agents, realtors, financial consultants, coaches, trainers, speakers, mortgage brokers, network marketers. All of these people can easily find value in having someone schedule their appointments, update posts on social media, check messages, schedule meetings, set up webinars, set up conference calls, update websites, enter data, and make various types of flyers or posters.

The main methods of marketing will be word of mouth and referrals. Be sure they keep their own business cards with them and hand one out to each customer.

Your child may also want to create a simple flyer that they can take to agents in your local area with a list of the services they provide, the days they are available to work, and your home phone number. Consider at what age you would allow your child to put their own cell phone number on the flyer. It should mention their attention to detail and any experience they have in the areas they provide service in. Use of color to grab people's attention in the flyer is a great idea; they can print on colored paper or use full color images.

Don't forget they can market online, too. Posting to their Facebook, Twitter, and Instagram accounts that they are now the proud owner of their own business is a good start.

Finances

Help your child create a PayPal account so that it's easier for professionals to pay them. Some people may also want to pay by check, so having a bank account may be helpful.

At the end of the project, help them track their earnings in a spreadsheet or manual table.

If you provided the money for their equipment or photo account membership fees, have them pay you back from the proceeds of their projects.

Make sure to help them split their money into the money envelope or bag system appropriately. Cost of supplies for future car washes should be set aside as short term savings. If they're old enough, they can open a savings account at the bank and make regular deposits in order to earn interest.

Business Plan for a Candy Shop

This business is perfect for kids aged 7 – 17 years old.

Mission Statement: To provide a neighborhood or event 'store' with candy kids can afford to buy.

Goals and Objectives: The goal is to create a business that provides a good source of income by working weekends, afternoons, and nights at events throughout the year. The objective is to compete with other vendors by offering popular candy and drinks at a low price.

Marketing: Work with event coordinators, sporting events, yard sales, etc. to be approved for selling at various venues throughout the year. Hand out business cards wherever appropriate to find future opportunities.

Competitive strengths are the low prices and convenience of this candy shop.

Pricing structure varies according to cost of goods sold but generally will start at $0.25 and go on up to $1.50 per item (easily affordable for kids with an allowance).

What this business teaches – How to make change, sales, planning in advance, customer service.

How we've used this plan – Our oldest son has done this business with quite a bit of success, although his venue created some issues and his business was shut down. Under the right circumstances, this is a great business!

Operational Plan

Inventory: What They'll Need

- Candy
  - o Laffy Taffy
  - o Tic-Tacs
  - o Snickers
  - o Twix
  - o Milky Way
  - o Hot Tamales
  - o Nerds
  - o Hershey Bar
  - o 3 Musketeers
  - o M&Ms
  - o Skittles
  - o Starburst
  - o Butterfinger
  - o 100 Grand
  - o Big Hunk
  - o Heath Bar
  - o Reese's
  - o Baby Ruth
  - o Pay Day
  - o Airheads
  - o Sugar Daddies
  - o Dots
  - o Almond Joy
  - o Tootsie Pops
  - o Licorice
  - o Gummy bears
  - o Lemon Heads
  - o Tootsie Rolls
  - o Mr. Goodbar
  - o Altoids
  - o Life Savers
  - o Chiclets
  - o Junior Mints
  - o Now & Laters
  - o Kit Kat
  - o Mounds
  - o Milk Duds
  - o Red Hots
  - o Sweet Tarts
  - o Bit-o-Honey
  - o Blow Pops
  - o Jolly Ranchers
  - o Crunch Bar
  - o Pop Tarts

- Ice cream bars, Otter Pops, ice cream sandwiches, etc.
- Gum
- Pop, Gatorade, Powerade, hot chocolate (if the weather is cold)
- Water, Vitamin Water, Propel

- Ice Chest
- 10-20 lbs crushed or block ice
- Card table
- Folding Chair
- Money box or envelope
- Change
- Price Signs
- Candy List (optional)

What to Do – Preparation

Help your child think about where they should set up their candy shop. It should be anywhere that people are going to get thirsty or hungry but don't want to or can't leave. Sporting events and garage sales are great because people usually don't think about bringing something to eat or drink, but they get hot and hungry.

They'll start by going shopping to purchase their supplies. Make sure they store the drinks in the fridge and the ice cream in a deep freezer so that they stay frozen hard until you take them to the event.

One of the first business decisions they'll have to make is how they are going to price their candy. If they buy it in bulk, they can buy it pretty inexpensively. They may want to price it reasonably low so that they'll have a lot of volume. It's good to have some candy priced at $0.25, $0.50, $1.00, and $1.50. This way, different kids in the same family will buy their own candy and people will buy more than one at a time.

Once they decide on pricing, they'll need to print up the price signs. Use a standard font like Times New Roman and a size of 275 points to create one sign per price. They are large so that they can put each one in front of a section of candy that is all one price. They may also want to print the customized list with the price of each. Your child should think about what they're saving the money for so they can tell people if they ask.

What to Do – On the Job

Next up is getting it all ready and out the door. They'll load up all their candy in a box and put the drinks and ice cream into the cooler with the ice. If it's hot in your area, they may consider putting the candy bars that might melt into the cooler too.

Make sure you get to the event early so that they can set up at a prime location. This is going to be where people are entering and exiting the event and can see them and you easily.

Tell them to have fun! Smile and talk to people as they go by. Your child should be outgoing and chat up prospective customers, telling them what they are trying to accomplish.

How to Make it Safe

Be within eyesight of your child in case they don't know how to answer a question and to ensure that they are safe.

Marketing Plan

Marketing will start by contacting the people in charge of various events and venues, such as coaches for team sports, neighbors holding yard sales, business owners, etc. Your child should pay attention to signs in your neighborhood advertising upcoming events and activities and write down the phone number to call the person in charge. It is best to contact as many people in advance as possible in order to create an appointment calendar for the next several months. They should always check with the event coordinator if it is okay to set up their shop; some towns and organizations have strict laws regarding where and what you can sell.

They should remember to keep their business cards handy at all times. It's a good idea to give them out to their customers and anyone they encounter at stores, school, church, etc. who might have need of their candy shop at their next event.

Online marketing is also appropriate. They should post to their Facebook, Twitter or Instagram account that they are now the proud owner of their own business and ask their friends and followers to notify them of any upcoming events where they could set up shop.

Finances

Your next-generation businessperson should keep track of inventory cost and their earnings in a spreadsheet or a manual table so you'll both know how much they can earn, and how much they have made. These should be tracked by activity and events so they can decide where their time is best spent. When they review this table later they can easily see which types of events are most profitable – and which are probably not worth their time.

Purchasing supplies when they are on sale or going to a warehouse club to get the best price is a great idea too. It's a good idea to buy packages that have a variety of candies so that you don't have to buy as many. It might be cheaper to order candy in bulk online, especially if you don't have a big warehouse or discount store in your town. Dollar stores are good choices, too.

If you provided the money for their supplies, have them pay you back from these proceeds. You may also want to charge for the gas it takes you to drive them to the events if you want them to bear the full cost.

Make sure to help them split their money into the money envelope or bag system appropriately. Cost of supplies for future candy sales should be set aside as short term savings. They can also start watching for when supply items come on sale to reduce their upfront costs and increase their profit margin. If they're old enough, they can open a savings account at the bank and make regular deposits in order to earn interest.

Business Plan for a Party DJ

General Description

This business is perfect for kids aged 13 – 17 years old.

Mission Statement: To provide entertainment for special occasions.

Goals and Objectives: The goal is to create a part-time business that provides a good source of income by working weekends, afternoons, and nights as available throughout the year. The objective is to build a business that can expand and extend into college years, while building a reputation for reliability and professionalism.

Marketing: This service will be marketed to neighbors, friends, church members, and extended family members who are planning a celebration for a special occasion such as a birthday party, neighborhood block party, or sports team victory event.

Competitive strengths are the cost, availability, and reliability of the service.

Pricing structure varies according to location and the duration of each event, but should be well below the professional DJ rate.

What this business teaches – Responsibility, reliability, how to create/maintain inventory, how to organize, and how to service a diverse demographic.

How we've used this plan – None of our kids have personally done this business, but we've hired teen DJs for parties that we've thrown in the past, and they worked out well.

Operational Plan

Inventory: What They'll Need

- Tabletop stereo system, or iPod with speakers
- Karaoke machine (optional)
- Turntable, mixer, headphones (optional)
- A wide assortment of music genres in mp3 or CD format
- Extension cord(s)
- Disco ball (optional)
- Fun lighting, such as strobes (optional)

What to Do – Preparation

Practicing with their friends first really is your child's first step. They should invite them over for a small party and provide the music. This is a good way to start because they already know the genre of music they prefer. The key is putting tunes together in a pleasing manner; they shouldn't play a hard rock song followed by a slow country ballad. As a DJ they need to try to get their friends up and moving, dancing, and having a good time. A good DJ will tell stories or talk about music trivia in between sets and get the crowd excited to hear the next song.

Learning to be a great DJ means planning their 'sets'. Planning a 'set' means developing blocks of songs with a similar theme, beat, or rhythm. Next they'll record and keep the lists in a notebook so they'll know ahead of time what music they will be playing and have sets of comparable length and style.

Using iTunes software or something similar to transfer songs to a CD or playlists on a laptop will also let them see how long each set is, time wise.

If they are thinking of using a karaoke machine, they'll want to print up a list of the available songs and keep that in a separate binder so guests can page through it. They will also need postcards or a notebook where the audience can indicate their song choice and be placed in the waiting line.

Since they are just starting out, they will need to charge less than DJs with lots of experience and fancy equipment. Come up with an hourly rate based on what others in your community are charging, and then divide that by half. They could also charge a set fee for a job up to four hours.

They may want to get a container, such as a large tote or plastic tub, to put all of their equipment, notebooks, and music in. This will make it easier to transport. The place where they are performing should provide a table and chair for them to set up; if not they will have to invest in a folding table and chair to bring with them.

To promote the new business they should make up flyers that include their name, the days and hours they're available, the type of equipment they are using along with any optional extras, their contact information, and their rate of pay. Specify the types of music they have in their inventory such as rock, alternative, etc. It is important to make the flyers professional but fun. Adding some graphics like music notes, images of people dancing, etc. will help make the flyers stand out.

When they get a call for a job from someone they don't personally know, it's important to find out how the caller heard about your child's new business. Make sure to get their name, address, and phone number.

When they take a job, they need to find out how many people are expected to attend the event, what hours they'll be working, when they can start setting up their equipment, and if the customer will be providing transportation to or from the event.

What to Do – On the Job

They should start by finding a corner of the main room or

outdoor space to set up their equipment. They don't want to be in the middle of the flow of traffic, but they do want people to see them so they know where to put in song requests. If they are using lights or a disco ball, asking the customer about their preferred placement is a great customer service and safety point. They may need help finding electrical outlets and in hanging lights which is a good opportunity for you to help them in set-up.

They will need to learn to match the music to the event. If it's a child's birthday party, for instance, they will want to play songs the kids can understand and that are popular with that particular age group.

They should definitely take a break between sets. Letting prearranged music play is a great way to keep the party going while they get a drink and relax for a few minutes.

They may want to keep a good supply of bottled water in a small ice chest nearby to make it easy to stay hydrated while they're working.

At the end of their gig, they get to pack up their equipment and leave the area neat and clean. Before they leave, they should ask for a referral from their customer.

How to Make It Safe

Don't let them accept any jobs where there will only be adults at the event or if alcohol will be served.

Go with your child to the event and check it out beforehand to ensure that it is a safe environment. Offer to help with electrical connections and setup.

Marketing Plan

The main methods of marketing will be word of mouth, referrals, and flyers posted in your neighborhood. At the end of each DJ gig, your child should offer business cards that their satisfied clients can share with other people they know.

They will want to spread the word of their business to school mates, your church congregation, relatives, neighbors, and friends. Make sure they keep their business cards and flyers handy at all times to give out when the opportunity presents itself. Keeping an eye out for notice of special events in your community or neighborhood is a good way for them to be proactive about getting work by approaching the organizers and offering their services.

Online marketing is good, too. They should post to their Facebook and/or Twitter account that they are now the proud owner of their own business. They should also let their friends and followers know they are available for DJ jobs but should never post the specifics of where they will be on their next gig. Suggest that they ask their friends and followers to notify them of any upcoming events where their services might be needed.

Finances

Satisfied customers will normally give them a tip if they think they have done an exceptional job – and congratulate your child on exceeding their customers' expectations. They can also place a small tip jar on their table while working; most people will add to it when they request a song.

Keep track of their earnings and expenses in a spreadsheet or a manual table so you both know how much they can earn, and how much they have made. Be sure to include the amount of any tips – these are customers they will want to go out of their way to work for again and again.

If you provided the money for their equipment, have them pay you back from these proceeds. You may also want to charge for the gas it takes you to drive them to get parties if you want them to bear the full cost.

Make sure to help them split their money into the money envelope or bag system appropriately. When they have made a profit, they might want to reinvest the money back into their business by buying new or additional equipment in order to expand – especially if this is a business they want to keep in the future. Your child can also open a savings account at the bank and make regular deposits in order to earn interest.

Business Plan for Sports Coaching

General Description

This business is perfect for kids aged 13 – 17 years old.

Mission Statement: To teach kids how to play a sport safely but competitively.

Goals and Objectives: The goal is to create a part-time business that provides a good source of income by working weekends, afternoons, and nights as available throughout the year. The objective is to form a business that provides a valuable service, while building a reputation for reliability and professionalism.

Marketing: This service will be marketed to neighbors, friends, church members, and extended family members who have school-aged children interested in sports or already playing in a league.

Competitive strengths are the cost, availability, and reliability of the service.

Pricing structure will be an hourly rate, but should be well below the professional instructor's rate.

What this business teaches: Responsibility, reliability, customer service, teaching skills, and patience.

How we've used this plan – We have hired teens to help our kids sharpen sports skills in the past and have enjoyed the results.

Operational Plan

Inventory: What They'll Need

- Their own sports equipment
  - Soccer balls
  - Baseballs/bats/gloves
  - Football
  - Volleyball
  - Basketball/hoop
  - Skateboard
  - Bicycle

- Items that can be used to mark off a field, serve as goals or nets, etc.
- Knee, elbow or shin pads
- Cones
- Safety equipment
- Goggles
- Clothing
- Workout wear
- Appropriate shoes
- Athletic cup (boys)
- Helmet
- Stopwatch/timer
- Bottled water
- Lesson plan
- Yard or field of appropriate size
- CPR lessons/certification
- First aid kit

What to Do – Preparation

First, they will need to find a place where lessons can be held. This might be in your backyard, their school recess area after hours, the YMCA, or a public sports field or park. They just need to be sure that it will always be available at the times they schedule lessons. Some sports, such as basketball, racquetball, or swimming will obviously require a location with the right equipment already in place.

Your child will have to plan out their lessons beforehand. Deciding how much time is needed to effectively teach a child to play a sport or to play it more competitively is a great exercise. This might be once a week for several months, for example.

They should plan a time period convenient for several children so they can teach a group rather than just an individual child. This works best for team sports but not so well for swimming, skateboarding, or other individual sports that require them to keep a close eye on the student.

Have them create a schedule on a calendar. If they are giving individual weekly lessons, they probably won't have time to work with more than one or two students at a time. Planning for family vacations and other times they won't be available is important and they should arrange to make up for that hole by adding a lesson to the end of the block.

They will want to print up flyers that include their name, days and hours they're available, the type of sports they are teaching, and their contact information (phone number and email address only), and their rate of pay. Teach your child to make the flyers professional but fun. Add some graphics like sports equipment, images of people playing, etc. to make them stand out.

When they get a job from someone they don't personally know, find out how they heard about your child's business. Make sure you and your child get their name, address, and phone number. Your budding capitalist should ask them where they expect the lessons to take place and if they will provide transportation.

What to Do – On the Job

Get the field of play set up early with goals, nets, boundaries, etc. They might have to walk off distances, or use a long measuring tape to get the proper size.

Ensure that their student is wearing the appropriate gear to stay safe. If not, have your child speak with the parents about the importance of providing the right apparel and accessories and ask them to purchase the necessities. You should not allow *your* child to start lessons until *their* child is wearing them.

It is up to your child to make sure the child they are teaching stays focused and pays attention to the lesson. Encourage them to be creative; make it fun. If they are putting the student through a timed drill, for instance, they might want to bring along a portable music system and play a song. They should ask the child to keep going until the music ends.

Each child will learn at their own rate. Your son or daughter will learn to adjust their lessons to match the child's ability level and talent.

If they are working with a group, they need to make sure that everyone gets a chance to play various positions and use all the equipment. One of the most important things they can do is to encourage kids who are struggling; they can't allow others to make fun of those who are having a harder time.

They should also take a short break midway through the lesson. Both them and their student need to stay hydrated – they need to make sure there is always fresh water available. If it is really hot, limit lessons to shorter time periods and ensure there is shade nearby where everyone can rest.

Both you and your child need to keep an eye out for any signs of physical distress. Stop the lesson immediately if you feel the student(s) is in any sort of danger.

At the end of the lesson, they need to pack up their equipment and leave the area neat and clean.

They may want to present a certificate of completion/achievement at the end of the course of lessons. It can easily be created using a computer and printer and a form they can buy, or simply printed on a colored sheet of paper listing the course name, the child's name, the date, and a signature line for the instructor.

How to Make it Safe

Accompany your child to each lesson. Keep an eye out for brewing fights, signs of physical distress, injury, or any other danger. Have your cell phone handy.

Marketing Plan

The main methods of marketing will be word of mouth, referrals, and flyers posted in your neighborhood. They can also approach any players on school or community teams and ask if they would like extra, individualized lessons. They should give them one of their business cards to take home to their parents. Asking your local sporting goods store if they can post a flyer on their bulletin board is another great promotional idea.

They should spread the word of their business to school mates, your church congregation, relatives, neighbors, and friends. Remind them to keep their business cards and flyers handy at all times to give out when the opportunity presents itself.

Online marketing is good, too. They should post to their Facebook and/or Twitter account that they are now the proud owner of their own business. They can let their friends and followers know they are available for sports lessons and ask them for leads, but don't let them post the specifics of their home address or where the lessons will take place for safety reasons.

Finances

Your budding business professional will want to provide a payment plan for their customers – either payment at the end of each lesson or a monthly amount that can be collected beforehand. Expect satisfied customers to give them a tip if they think they have done an exceptional job – and congratulate your child on exceeding their customers' expectations.

It may be more convenient for some customers to pay them with a check. You may want to help them cash the checks at the bank or set up their own account so they can deposit them.

This is a business they can continue throughout school and even during college. If so, they will want to reinvest some of their earnings in additional or upgraded equipment.

Business Plan for Musical/Singing Lessons

This business is perfect for kids aged: 13 – 17 years old.

Mission Statement: To teach kids how to play an instrument or sing.

Goals and Objectives: The goal is to create a part-time business that provides a good source of income by working weekends, afternoons, and nights as available throughout the year. The objective is to form a business that can expand and extend into college years, while building a reputation for reliability and professionalism.

Marketing: This service will be marketed to neighbors, friends, church members, and extended family members who have school-aged children interested in music.

Competitive strengths are the cost, availability, and reliability of the service.

Pricing structure will be an hourly rate, but should be well below the professional instructor's rate.

What this business teaches – Responsibility, reliability, customer service, teaching skills, patience.

How we've used this plan – We have not personally used this plan because Jill has helped out kids with music lessons.

Operational Plan

Inventory: What They'll Need

- Their own instrument
- Karaoke machine with microphone (optional for singing lessons)
- Electronic or manual tuner
- Sheet music
- Music stand
- Lesson plan
- Homework assignments

What to Do – Preparation

To start with, they will need to come up with a standard lesson package, say once a week, for an hour at a time, for a six-month period.

This will lead them to create a lesson plan for the beginning musician or singer. They may need to adjust this after they begin working with each student to match the child's skill level. Some kids will learn quickly while others will have a harder time. Organizing their lessons in a three-ring binder makes it easier to transport.

Your child will make assignments for the student to complete on his or her own each week. It is a good idea to have them get a student folder where they can keep their weekly homework assignments.

The instructor will want to make copies of the songs they will be teaching so the student can have his own copy in front of him while learning.

They will also have to figure out where to hold lessons. It may be a spare room in your home or they could offer to teach at the student's house if it is someone you know well who lives nearby. Of course, if they are teaching piano lessons, they will have to give lessons at your house, unless the student has his or her own piano at home. Remember the noise factor; they will want to try to find a spot that won't disturb others.

Encourage them to create a schedule on a calendar. If they are giving weekly lessons, they probably won't have time to work with more than one or two students at a time. They will also have to plan for family vacations, holidays, and other times they won't be available.

Have them make up flyers that include their name, the days and hours they're available, the type of instruments/music they are teaching along with their contact information (phone number (non-cell) and email address only), and their rate of pay. Help them make the flyers professional but fun. Add some graphics like music notes, clip art of people playing an instrument, etc. to make them stand out.

When they get a job from someone they don't personally know, find out how they heard about your child's business. Have your child make sure to get their name, address, and phone number. It is important that they ask them where they expect the lessons to take place and if the customer will provide transportation.

What to Do – On the Job

They'll have to set up their music stand, stool (if needed), and sheet music – or karaoke machine if they are giving singing lessons. Next they will get the student situated with his own instrument and sheet music and they can begin with some warm-up exercises before going into the lesson.

It is up to them to make sure the child they are teaching stays focused and pays attention to the lesson. It should be something creative; make it fun and teach the kind of music the child likes best to help keep and drive their interest.

Each child will learn at their own rate. Your child will have to adjust their lessons to match the child's ability level and talent.

The instructor should test the student each week on what they learned in the previous lesson and enlist the parent's help ensuring that homework assignments are done; they may even ask the parent to sign off on completion.

At the end of the lesson, pack up your equipment and leave the area neat and clean.

How to Make It Safe

Accompany your child to the first lesson or so outside your home to ensure it is a safe environment.

Marketing Plan

The main methods of marketing will be word of mouth, referrals, and flyers posted in your neighborhood. They can also approach any beginning band students in their school and ask if they would like lessons. Encourage them to give the kids one of their business cards to take home to their parents. They can also ask your local music store if they can post a flyer on their bulletin board.

They should make every effort to spread the word of their business to school mates, your church congregation, relatives, neighbors, and friends and always keep their business cards and flyers handy at all times to give out when the opportunity presents itself.

Online marketing is good, too. Your child should post to their Facebook and/or Twitter account that they are now the proud owner of their own business and let their friends and followers know they are available for music lessons. One important point though; they should never post the specifics of their address or cell phone number.

Finances

It's very important that your child provide a payment plan for their customers – either payment at the end of each lesson or a monthly amount with specific due date (either payable in advance or at the last lesson of the month). Expect satisfied customers to give them a tip if they think they have done an exceptional job – and congratulate your child on exceeding their customers' expectations.

It may be more convenient for some customers to pay them with a check. You may wish to help your child cash the checks at the bank or set up their own account so they can deposit them.

This is a business they can continue throughout school and even during college. If so, they will want to reinvest some of their earnings in additional or upgraded equipment.

Business Plan for a Babysitting Service

General Description

This business is perfect for kids aged 11 – 17 years old.

Mission Statement: To provide reliable, trustworthy babysitting service for parents with young children.

Goals and Objectives: The goal is to create a business that provides a good source of income by working weekends, afternoons, and nights throughout the year. The objective is to build a reputation for trustworthiness and obtain repeat clientele.

Marketing: This service will be marketed to neighbors, friends, church members, and extended family members with young children.

Competitive strengths are the honesty, reliability, and trustworthiness of the babysitter.

Pricing structure varies according to location and competition.

What this business teaches – Responsibility, child care, the importance of being punctual.

How we've used this plan – All of our girls have used this business plan with great success. They have made hundreds, if not thousands, of dollars babysitting.

Operational Plan

Inventory: What They'll Need

- CPR and First Aid training (optional but highly recommended)
- Babysitting training class (optional but recommended)
- List of emergency numbers in your area
- Fun Bag or Box
- Age appropriate movies
- Crayons, Coloring Books
- Stickers, Card games (Uno, Go Fish, etc.)
- Crafts
- Candy (if allowed)
- Colored paper and a printer

What to Do – Preparation

It's important for your child to get the proper training like they would with any other business. They should strongly consider taking a CPR, First Aid, or babysitting class through your local Red Cross or Parks and Recreation department. This will help them feel more comfortable if they've never babysat before and will be a selling point for the parents.

There's no set rate to charge for sitting, so find out what the going rate is for babysitting in your area. Your child can ask you (their parents), friends, or relatives who babysit what they charge. They may consider lowering their rate if there's a lot of competition for babysitting or they may charge the same rate but include light housekeeping at no charge.

Next, they can put together a 'fun bag.' It' is important to make sure to include things that are appropriate for all ages.

They should make up flyers that include their name, the days and hours they're available, their experience level and training, references, their contact information, and their rate of pay if they have a set amount. If they're going to do light housekeeping, add this as well. This is where they can make it professional but fun. They should also include that they have fun activities for kids of all ages. Get your kid to hand these out to people they know from church, their younger siblings' friends, your friends, and people in the neighborhood.

When they get a job, find out how they heard about your child if they don't personally know them. Make sure to get their name, address, and phone number. Also find out how many kids they'll be watching, what hours they'll be working, and if they'll be picking your child up or if you're expected to give them a ride there.

What to Do – On the Job

Encourage your child to have the parents show them the doors and windows and how they lock. Have them explain any alarm system. Your child should find out where the first aid supplies and fire extinguisher are stored. They should also be sure to ask if there are any special instructions like nap or bed times, using the TV or radio, and whether they can play outside or cook.

It's important to always watch the children so they don't get hurt or make messes. Your child should not leave them alone in order to do the cleaning.

If they hear suspicious noises, if someone comes to the door requesting to use the phone and won't leave, or if they receive unusual or obscene calls, they should call the police immediately. They should not go outside to check things out and they should never let people into the house.

In case of fire, they need to get the children outside and call the fire department from a neighbor's house.

It's also important to play games with the children that they enjoy. They won't have as much fun if your child just sits and watches. They need to get involved with them. Suggest they let the kids help them with the cleaning. They can pick up toys and books. Most children like washing dishes. Be sure that they take any sharp objects out of the sink first.

When the kids get bored, they can pull out the fun bag and do some of the activities in it. If they don't want to play with these objects anymore, great games they can play include 'follow the leader' or 'Simon Says.'

When Parents Get Back

Firstly, your child should let the parents know what they did, including anything that was unusual. Either they should be sure that the customer provides a ride home after dark, or they should call you for a ride. Your child should know that if the customer appears intoxicated, to call you to come and get them.

It's important to stress to your child to thank customers for the opportunity to babysit their children and let them know they'd like to do it again. They may even ask them to be a reference for your child in the future.

How to Make It Safe

One good way is to encourage your child to only give their babysitting flyer to families who have children. This helps you stay safe.

Marketing Plan

The main methods of marketing will be word of mouth, referrals, and flyers posted in your neighborhood. At the end of each babysitting job, offer business cards that their satisfied clients can share with other parents they know.

Your child can spread the word of their business to school mates, your church congregation, relatives, neighbors, and friends. Again, encourage them to keep their business cards and flyers handy at all times to give out when the opportunity presents itself. They can also remember to talk to the parents of their brother's or sister's friends. They may want to hire your child when they meet with teachers or need a night out alone and since they already know your family, they are a shoe-in for the job.

Online marketing is good, too. Make sure they post to their Facebook and/or Twitter account that they are now the proud owner of their own business. It's vital to let their friends and followers know they are available for babysitting, but they should never give out the specifics, such as for whom they'll be working, or when, and where their next job is going to be.

Finances

Expect parents to give them a tip if they think they have done an exceptional job – and congratulate your child on exceeding their customers' expectations.

Keep track of their earnings and expenses in a spreadsheet or a manual table so you'll both know how much they can earn, and how much they have made. Be sure to include the amount of any tips – these are customers they will want to go out of their way to work for again and again.

If you provided the money for their fun bag supplies, have them pay you back from the proceeds of their first job. You may also want to charge for the gas it takes you to drive them to their babysitting job if you want them to bear the full cost.

Make sure to help them split their money into the money envelope or bag system appropriately. Cost of supplies for more games should be set aside as short term savings. If they're old enough, they can open a savings account at the bank and make regular deposits in order to earn interest.

Business Plan for a Pet Washing/Grooming Service

General Description

This business is perfect for kids aged 10 – 17 years old.

Mission Statement: To provide a service to busy people who don't have time to wash and groom their pets.

Goals and Objectives: The goal is to create a business that provides a good source of income during the summer months and weekends throughout the year. The objective is to build a reputation for caring service, attention to detail, and reliability.

Marketing: The pet washing and grooming service will be marketed as a way for busy working people to have someone else take care of their pets' needs, saving time.

Competitive strengths are in convenience to the customer and value pricing.

Pricing structure is a set fee for the service, dependent on the number of services desired. Develop a rate structure for varying packages.

What this business teaches – Reliability, customer service, caring for animals, and handling money.

How we've used this plan – None of our kids have yet used this business plan. However, I'm sure some of the boys will soon!

Operational Plan

Inventory & Supplies: What They'll Need

- Large plastic tub
- Hose with sprayer attachment
- Pet shampoo
- Old towels
- Pet brush
- Scissors
- Dog and cat treats

What to Do – Preparation

To get the word out, it's important that your child targets neighbors, friends' families, extended family members, church members, and senior citizens. They can start by making up a flyer with their business name and rates. They can advertise that they will go to the home to wash and groom cats, dogs, or other small animals.

They should organize all their supplies in the large tub so they are easily transported.

You may need to help to handle larger dogs. Have them ask a parent or sibling to accompany them, and help keep a large animal still while washing and grooming.

What to Do – On the Job

It is always a good idea for your child to ask the customer if the animal has had all its shots before beginning. They should also ask if the owner prefers they use regular shampoo or one that prevents fleas and ticks.

They really should work outside when weather permits. It it's cold, they can see if they can use the owner's bathtub for bathing inside the house.

It's important for your child to keep the animal calm while they are working. They should leave the collar on so they have something to hold onto. For a thorough wash, they should scrub down into the skin with the shampoo. They need to also be careful not to get soap into the animal's eyes.

Once the animal is all lathered up, they should rinse the animal well, getting down to the skin, and towel dry.

When they brush the fur they should use scissors to carefully cut out any bad matting or weeds stuck in the fur. Remind them to be gentle as some animals don't like this or may feel pain when the brush encounters a tangle.

How to Make it Safe

Never let them wash and groom an animal that shows signs of illness or bad temper.

Don't let them offer to clip nails or fur – this could be dangerous if the animal doesn't like it or your hand slips. They could start bleeding.

It's also a good idea for you to help your child as necessary and transport/accompany them to each job.

Marketing Plan

The main method of marketing will be flyers and word of mouth to family members, schoolmates, friends, church members, etc. They should post their flyer at a veterinary office, the animal shelter, the bulletin board at a senior community (lots of older people have small dogs and cats for companionship), the grocery store, and throughout your neighborhood. Remind them to always ask permission when posting at a business.

Encourage them to be sure to take their business cards with them and hand one out to each customer so they can spread the word. Another great way to drum up more business is to ask customers for referrals.

They can also take a walk in your neighborhood. Any time they see pets in a yard, they can leave a flyer on the front door or in the mailbox.

Another idea would be to hold a neighborhood dog wash on a specific weekend. They can invite their friends, neighbors, and family members to bring their pets. All they need to do is to ask for a donation for each animal they wash. They can advertise this with a small classified ad in your local newspaper or hold it in conjunction with a neighborhood yard sale.

Finances

Keep track of their earnings and expenses so you both know how much they are making. If they receive a tip, include that amount, too.

Their money will earn interest if they open a savings account at the bank and make regular deposits.

If they like this type of work and want to continue, they may consider taking classes on professional grooming techniques. This will also teach them how best to handle difficult pets safely.

Business Plan for Jewelry Making & Sales

General Description

This business is perfect for kids aged 10 – 17 years old.

Mission Statement: To offer unique, handmade, or custom jewelry that is affordable.

Goals and Objectives: The goal is to create a part-time business that provides a good source of income by creating jewelry outside of school hours. The objective is to use creativity in making the items for sale, while competing with retail stores for customers.

Marketing: Team up with neighbors holding yard sales as a venue for selling their jewelry and/or go door-to-door. Hand out business cards wherever appropriate to find future opportunities.

Competitive strengths are the low prices and convenience of this jewelry "store".

Pricing structure varies according to cost of materials used but should be well below retail store pricing and easily affordable for kids with an allowance.

What this business teaches – How to be creative, make change, sales, planning in advance, customer service.

How we've used this plan – One of our daughters loved using this business plan to earn spending money and to enjoy crafting jewelry.

Inventory: What They'll Need

- Jewelry making items (if your town doesn't have a craft store, they can find supplies online)
  - o Beads of various shapes, sizes, materials, colors
  - o Leather cord in various colors
  - o Transparent fishing line
  - o Findings (for earrings, necklace clasps, pins, etc.)
  - o Fine elastic
- A box with compartments to store your finished pieces
- Money box or envelope
- Coins and bills for change
- Price list
- Order forms (optional)

What to Do – Preparation

They will need to create a good inventory of jewelry before they start selling. If they don't have a lot of experience making jewelry, they might want to start with a kit that contains everything they'll need to learn the basics. This is where they need to experiment with their creativity and create pieces that they and their friends would like, but they should also consider making some pieces that adults would wear, too.

They may want to try to purchase their supplies in bulk to get the best price. They should try to buy a lot of different colors and textures of supplies unless they want to specialize in a certain style.

Next they should think about how they are going to price their jewelry. Encourage them to take into account the cost of supplies along with their time. You may want to visit a retail store with them and note their prices. The more reasonable their prices are, the more sales they will make to kids who are using their allowance to buy it.

They also need to print up a price sheet. They can post this inside their container or simply print them up on pages that they can hand out to customers.

What to Do – On the Job

For display, they will want to place their jewelry in the container in a way that makes it easy to see each piece. They may want to line each section of the box with felt so the jewelry stays in place. Use a straight pin to fasten necklaces or earrings to the felt.

Suggest your child go door-to-door in your neighborhood or set up a table at a yard sale or craft fair. They could also ask stores to take their jewelry on consignment and leave a display on the counter.

A great way to break the ice and generate sales is to have your child ask their customers if there are any birthdays or special events coming up – they may want to order additional jewelry as gifts. Sometimes asking them reminds them of upcoming events they might have forgotten.

They can also ask people if they want custom jewelry made (they will want to print an order form if they will be making custom pieces), especially if the customer doesn't see anything in their inventory that they like.

Remind your child to be sure to save money from their sales to repay the upfront costs of the supplies and to replenish them. On a good sales day, they might just sell out!

How to Make it Safe

Accompany your child if he or she is going door-to-door to sell jewelry.

Price List

They can copy this list as is or put it into an Excel spreadsheet.

Jewelry Making

Price

	Price
Bracelet	
Ring	
Earrings	
Necklace	
Anklet	
Toe Ring	
Band	
Sets	
Cell Phone Dangle	
Special Order	

Special Order Form

Name	
Address	
Phone Number	
Description	
Price	
Deposit Paid	
Delivery Date	

Marketing Plan

Creating flyers they can post in your neighborhood, at your church, or at school is a great low cost way to start promoting their business. They might want to include color photos of some of their completed pieces to really show them off. Holidays are a great time to advertise. They can prepare a special flyer with a

Mother's Day, Valentine's Day, or Christmas theme and hand them out wherever possible, such as at school, in your neighborhood, etc.

Your child should hand out business cards to make people aware of their jewelry sales. Remind them to talk to neighbors, their siblings' friends, people in your church, and classmates.

Partnering with neighbors having yard sales is another great way to get business; they should try to see if they can set up a table at their sale. Door-to-door sales work well, too. It's important to remember to pass out their business cards and flyers to each customer so they can spread the word.

Suggest that they host a jewelry party for their friends – either a sleepover or an afternoon tea with drinks and snacks. They can let their friends know in advance they'll be offering their jewelry for sale so they can bring their allowance.

Online marketing is also appropriate. Posting to their Facebook and/or Twitter account that they are now the proud owner of their own business is a great place to start. They can then ask their friends and followers to notify them of any upcoming events where they could set up shop. To add more content to their Facebook postings they can take pictures, with permission, of customers wearing their jewelry that they can post to their online photo gallery.

Finances

Keep track of inventory cost and their earnings and expenses in a spreadsheet or a manual table so you'll both know how much they can earn, and how much they have made. When you review this table later you both can easily see which types of jewelry are most popular and profitable – and which are probably not worth their time creating again.

A great way to lower costs is to have your child look for the best deals when buying their supplies. It might be cheaper to order their supplies in bulk online, especially if they don't have a craft store in your town. Dollar stores are good choices, too.

Their money will earn interest if they open a savings account at the bank and make regular deposits.

If you provided the money for the cost of their initial inventory, remind them to consider paying you back from the proceeds of their business. Let them know that you are sure to be impressed by their responsibility. They also need to remember to set aside some of their proceeds to pay for more inventory as necessary so they don't have to ask you for money again.

Business Plan for a Personal Shopping Service

This business is perfect for kids aged: 12 – 17 years old

Mission Statement: To provide a service to busy people who don't have time to shop for themselves:

Goals and Objectives: The goal is to create a business that provides a good source of income during the summer months and weekends throughout the year. The objective is to build a reputation for reliability, shopping savvy, and the ability to stay within a budget.

Marketing: Personal shopping service will be marketed as a way for busy working people to employ someone else to do the shopping for gifts, groceries, or other items.

Competitive strengths are in convenience to the customer and personalized customer service.

Pricing structure is a set fee for the service, on top of the cost of items being purchased.

What this business teaches – Reliability, organization, staying within budget, customer service, handling money, how to compare prices.

How we've used this plan – One of our daughters currently does this as a side business for people she babysits for. She has found it to be a great additional stream of income for existing clients.

Inventory & Supplies: What They'll Need

- Transportation
- Phone
- Interview form
- Binder for customer information
- Order form
- Shopping list

What to Do – Preparation

Targeting neighbors, family members, church members, and senior citizens, they should make up a flyer with a cute name for their business, such as "Annie the Shopper". On the flyer they can list out the types of things they will shop for and advertise their affordable rate for this service.

Their job is to find out what people need and what types of things they want. This starts with an interview, either in person or over the phone. There's a sample interview form at the end of this section they can use for reference.

Keeping a binder organized by customer name that contains the interview form with all their personal information and a record of all the orders they've placed is a great way of making it easier next time your child needs to go shopping for them again.

Your child's next step is to research the cost of the items requested. A good place to start is to look for sales and coupons online and in your local newspaper. Their customer will appreciate their research into finding the best deal.

It's always a good idea to obtain the customer's money up front so they don't have to use or borrow your money to upfront the purchase.

As the parent, it will probably be up to you to provide transportation so they should try to organize their jobs so that they can shop for more than one customer at a time; preferably at a mall or shopping center to limit travel time. If they make a list of the items they are shopping for and map out the stores they need to visit, it will save a lot of time. If they find a new store they've never visited before, it's helpful to the parent driving for your child to have driving directions.

If they will be shopping for a customer who needs something like groceries on a regular basis, be sure to create a calendar to keep track of the days they are scheduled to deliver the order.

What to Do – On the Job

Your child will have to learn to shop carefully to stay within budget and satisfy the customer's instructions.

By keeping all the receipts in their purse, fanny pack, or a folder to present to the customer, along with their change they will be able to go over them easily with the customer at delivery. They may be asked to return some items, so you will need the receipt for that, too.

If they are unsure about an item they find being what the customer wants, they can give them a call and ask or buy more than one option to give them a choice.

They should never be afraid to enlist the help of a sales clerk at the store. It will save time if they describe the item they are seeking and ask if the store carries it in stock. If not, they might be able to suggest an alternate store for your young shopper to visit.

Delivery

Perishable items, such as groceries, will need to be delivered to the customer immediately. For other types of items, they can make an appointment for delivery.

At the delivery they should bring the bags and boxes to their customer at their home or place of business. This will give them the chance to show their purchases one by one and make sure they approve. If not, your child may offer to return the items.

It is also wise for them to not have anything gift wrapped until the customer approves the purchase.

Providing receipts and change shows professionalism and builds trust encouraging the customer to use your young entrepreneur again.

How to Make it Safe

Help your child post flyers by placing them around your office or handing out to acquaintances. Accompany your child to in-person interviews. Provide transportation for their shopping trips and deliveries.

Interview Form

Name_____

Address_____

Contact Information_____

Favorite color_____

Colors/Styles in Home_____

_____

Spouse Name/Birthdate/Anniversary_____

_____

Family Members/Birthdates_____

_____

Additional Information_____

_____

Order Form

Item_____

Size/Color/Style_____

Description_____

Purpose of purchase (gift, self, etc.)_____

_____

IF GIFT:

Age of recipient _____ Favorite color _____

Gift wrapping?   Yes   No

Boy or girl? _____ Budget (maximum) _____

Money received _____ Date requested _____

Delivery date and time _____

Groceries (write-in list):

_____   _____

_____   _____

_____   _____

_____   _____

_____   _____

_____   _____

_____   _____

_____   _____

_____   _____

_____   _____

Tip: Keep copies of all lists so you can refer back to them to make future orders easier for your customer.

Marketing Plan

The main method of marketing will be flyers and word of mouth to family members, schoolmates, friends, church members, etc. They should post their flyer at the grocery store, the bulletin boards at a senior community, the senior citizens center, medical offices, and in neighborhood office buildings. Many older people or those with medical conditions find it difficult to shop for themselves.

Suggest your child take their business cards with them and hand one out to each customer when they deliver their order. They also should follow up by asking customers for referrals.

This is a business where it definitely is a great idea for your child to be friendly and approachable when they are out shopping. Offering assistance to elderly or handicapped shoppers and letting them know about their business may be a great way to earn new business. If they see someone who is obviously searching for the perfect gift, they really should offer to help them, too, and explain that this is their business.

Finances

This is the part where they need to keep careful track of the money they receive and how much change is owed back to their customer. It is a good idea to keep a log book and a separate place to store the money (like a money bag or fanny pack) until they have done their shopping. If they receive a tip, indicating that in their log book will let them know exactly how much they have earned.

This next point should be stressed seriously to your child: Never, ever, should they "borrow" any of their customer's money with the intent to pay it back. Waiting until they've made a profit before they buy something for themselves is the only way to do this job.

Their money will earn interest if they open a savings account at the bank and make regular deposits. Some people may want to pay them with a check so a bank account will make it easier to handle this form of payment.

As they get more experienced, they can then consider charging a bit more for their services – especially if they have a particularly picky customer who asks for lots of returns.

Business Plan for a Window Washing Service

This business is perfect for kids aged 8 – 17 years old.

Mission Statement: To provide a service to busy people or business owner who don't have time to wash windows.

Goals and Objectives: The goal is to create a business that provides a good source of income during the summer and on weekends. The objective is to build a reputation for value, attention to detail, and reliability.

Marketing: The window washing business will be marketed as a way for busy working people to have someone else take care of their windows, both inside and out. It will also be marketed to business owners who may need this service at their office.

Competitive strengths are saving the customer time and value pricing.

Pricing structure is a set fee for the service, dependent on the number of windows that need to be cleaned. Develop a rate structure for varying packages such as weekly, monthly, or one time.

What this business teaches – Reliability, customer service, and handling money.

How we've used this plan – None of our kids have used this plan, but we know teens that have done very well with it.

Operational Plan

Inventory & Supplies: What They'll Need

- Two pails
- Squeegee with telescoping handle
- Stepladder
- Garden hose with spray attachment
- Glass cleaner (they can make their own)
- Cornstarch
- Measuring cup (half cup)
- Coffee filters
- Newspapers
- Soft cotton rags or chamois cloth

Recipe #1 for Homemade Window Cleaning Solution

- Plain white vinegar
- Rubbing alcohol
- Half a lemon or bottled lemon juice
- Dishwashing liquid

Take an empty, clean spray container and fill it ¾ full with vinegar. Add rubbing alcohol until the container is almost full. Add juice of half lemon squeezed or about 1 tablespoon of bottled lemon juice. Finish off with a squirt of dishwashing liquid.

Recipe #2 for Homemade Window Cleaning Solution

- Pail of warm water
- ½ cup of cornstarch

Mix the cornstarch into the pail of water. Wipe on with a clean cloth and wipe off with wadded up newspaper pages.

What to Do – Preparation

Target neighbors, friends' families, extended family members, church members, senior citizens, and small business owners and have your child make up a flyer with their business name and rates. Advertise that they will go to the home to wash windows both inside and out. They can also go door-to-door to find customers.

They should place their supplies in the pails so they are easily transported.

They can buy their cleaning products or make their own. If they are using the cornstarch recipe, they should bring along a box of cornstarch and a measuring cup so they can mix it up on the spot for maximum effectiveness.

It's important that they do some research on the rates that professional window cleaners charge for their service. Their rate should be about half, and they should come up with a price for one-time, weekly, and monthly service – it's easier to keep windows clean if they do it on a regular basis.

What to Do – On the Job

Your child will ask the customer how often they would like their windows cleaned and quote the appropriate price. Businesses will probably want them to do the job daily or weekly, especially if they have glass doors that get lots of fingerprints on them.

Start with the outside of the windows. They can use one of those cleaners with a bottle that attaches to the hose to make this easier – especially if they are short and it's hard to reach the top of the window. If not, they will spray their homemade or commercial cleaner on the outside glass and use the squeegee to scrape it off and finish by polishing with their clean rag or chamois cloth. If they need it, they can also use a stepladder.

Next, they will move inside. If they are working in an office, they need to be careful not to disturb employees or customers.

The best way to clean interior glass is to mix up the cornstarch and water recipe and wipe it on the glass with one cloth, then take a clean cloth and dry it off. They can also use wadded up newspaper or coffee filters for the final wipe. They should definitely experiment with what works best depending on the type of dirt they encounter. The cornstarch formula works great for streaky glass but they might need the stronger vinegar recipe for getting rid of greasy dirt.

When they are finished, have them pack their supplies back into the pails and throw away their trash.

How to Make it Safe

Hold the stepladder steady for your child when using. Don't let him or her enter a stranger's home alone. Be sure the child knows how to handle cleaning chemicals safely.

Marketing Plan

The main method of marketing will be flyers and word of mouth sent to family members, schoolmates, friends, church members, etc. Have them post their flyer at the grocery store, the bulletin board at the local senior citizens center, and throughout your neighborhood.

Have them go to the office complexes near your house and drop off a flyer at each business.

Be sure to remind them to take their business cards with them and hand them out to customers so they can spread the word. They also should always ask customers for referrals.

They also can line up a lot of business just by going door-to-door in your neighborhood and offer their services.

Finances

Keep track of their earnings so you both know how much they are making, less the cost of supplies. If they receive a tip, include that amount, too.

Their money will earn interest if they open a savings account at the bank and make regular deposits.

If they like this type of work and want to expand, they may want to consider offering house cleaning services in addition to window washing.

About the Authors

David Teancum Fagan was born in 1976, in the Fort Hood Army Hospital in Killeen, Texas where his father Vernon Fagan Jr. was stationed. David is the oldest of six kids, with five younger sisters. Although David's family made a few significant moves as a kid, including a short time being stationed in what was once West Germany, David mostly grew up in various small towns in Oregon.

David left high school in the fall of his 11th grade year, opting for a GED and eventually moving out on his own when he was 17. He later went to some college classes at the University of Phoenix, paid for or reimbursed by his employer at the time, Wells Fargo Bank. Although he didn't graduate from Harvard, he also took courses there as part of a program for CEO's. David firmly believes in customizing an education and that traditional schooling isn't for everyone.

Jill grew up mostly in northern California and Arizona, the fourth of eight kids. Jill has always been a good fit for school, and she enjoys the process of learning. Jill graduated from Flagstaff High School in 1993, and went to Coconino Community College on a full scholarship. She was able to complete all of her pre-nursing classes and graduate with an Associate of Arts degree in two years. She then attended nursing school at Mesa Community College. When she met and married David, she dropped out of nursing school to be a full time mom.

David married Jill Packard in the late 90's, and together they have nine children but are raising eight due to one full term baby passing away during birth in January 2006. Jill has been pregnant nine times for nine months each, or about seven full years of the first 15 years they were together.

When David and Jill met, David had just passed the tests necessary to become an officer for the Phoenix Police Department. During the slow hiring process, David took a job at a bank and ended up being there for almost five years.

Since 1994, David has almost always been involved in sales and marketing. And since 2002, David has almost always worked for himself. His jobs and businesses have involved banking and real estate mostly until about 2007, when he reinvented himself in the world of business development, marketing, and publicity helping others grow their businesses.

Jill has worked mainly in quality control since college. She was a legal secretary for two attorneys, a quality control associate at an investment firm, and has always done the financials for David's companies.

Although David was mostly raised in Oregon, he believes he really found himself, started his family, and developed his talents while living in Arizona for roughly 12 years. Other than a lifestyle experiment of living in the Northwest on a 10 acre farm, David and Jill have most recently lived in Southern California.

Currently David and his family live in Laguna, California two miles from Dana Point Harbor where he keeps his sailboat. His family has moved a lot to accept opportunities and try out new adventures. David's kids have rarely gone to the same school for more than two years in a row.

Today, David T. Fagan is best known as a Speaker, Author, and Entrepreneur as the Icon Builder with his marketing and PR company based out of Beverly Hills, CA. He is the former CEO of Guerrilla Marketing, which sold over 23 million books in 62 languages all over the world. He's also the former owner of LCO Communications that has represented 58 Academy Award Winners, 34 Grammy Winners, and 43 New York Times Best Sellers.

About the Authors

David owns Icon Builder Media, is a guest lecturer at UCLA, and has been recently featured in Fox & Friends, The Washington Post, Forbes, The Today Show, Fox's the Five, Neil Cavuto, The Doctors Show, ABC's 20/20, Investor's Business Daily, Yahoo! News, The Wrap, and the Los Angeles Business Journal, and many more media outlets.

David is an International Speaker in places as far away as Bangladesh and Australia. David has shared the stage with Former Secretary of Defense Dr. Bob Gates, Mark Victor Hansen, Dan Kennedy, Harry Dent, and John Assaraf to name a few.

David loves to sail, play basketball, coach his kids, and bicycle. He has written several other books and is highly sought after to endorse other books and write and forewords. He recommends that parents also read his book, *From Invisible to Invincible: Discovering the Art of Being Heard, Being Seen, Getting Results and Gaining Wisdom.*

Jill has worked for attorneys, financial companies, and has personally handled the operations side of almost all of David's businesses. She is the organized, attentive to detail person that balances the risk taking and creative entrepreneurial life that David leads.

Jill has a love for alternative healing, home remedies, essential oils, and making tinctures with plants that have medicinal properties. She dreams of gardening once again someday but stays busy with her kids, helping out with David's company, and running a company of her own – On the Inside Press, a custom publishing company.

Jill's publishing company is a very successful boutique publishing house primarily helping experts like attorneys, doctors, dentists, real estate investors, coaches, corporate leaders, and trainers put out nonfiction books.

Jill owns more guns than David, is somewhat conservative, and believes in being prepared – complete with home canned foods, 72 hour kits, and storing other supplies that could be useful in an emergency.

David and Jill both agree that they are done having kids. They enjoy working and traveling together, living somewhat of a double life: part of the time at home with a bunch of kids and the other part going to seminars and parties in Beverly Hills and Hollywood.